GOD'S
END-TIME
CALENDAR

GOD'S END-TIME CALENDAR

ROD PARSLEY

CHARISMA
HOUSE

GOD'S END-TIME CALENDAR by Rod Parsley
Published by Charisma House
Charisma Media/Charisma House Book Group
600 Rinehart Road
Lake Mary, Florida 32746
www.charismahouse.com

Cover design by Eric Lopez
Design Directors: Justin Evans and Megan Hassett

Visit the author's website at www.rodparsley.com.

Library of Congress Control Number: 2015945056
International Standard Book Number: 978-1-62998-703-3
E-book ISBN: 978-1-62998-704-0

First edition

15 16 17 18 19 — 9 8 7 6 5 4 3 2 1
Printed in the United States of America

It is my honor to dedicate this book to my precious mother, Mrs. Ellen Parsley. Her love for the Lord, her faith in Him, and her hope in His appearing has been a true inspiration to me for nearly sixty years.

Her legacy is one of rich spiritual roots that run deep from the hills of eastern Kentucky where she was born and raised, to traveling to the continents of South America, Africa, Asia, and Europe to preach the unadulterated Word of God with power and conviction under the unction and anointing of the Holy Spirit.

I'm so thankful for the opportunity and sheer joy of being nurtured in a home where my mother and father put their love for God and His Word above all else. I can't ever remember missing a church service—for any reason. To this day whenever I visit my mother, she is studying the Word—surrounded by Bibles and study resources, and her television or news outlets and other electronic devices are tuned only to Christian channels!

Mom, as I lovingly call her, has always had a strong inclination toward the prophetic and end-time themes woven in God's Word as she anxiously awaits the return of our soon-coming King for His church. So it is with overwhelming pride that I wish to publicly express my sincere love and gratitude to her for instilling these truths and values in my life by dedicating this book to her.

I leave you with these words:

For the Lord Himself will descend from heaven with a shout, with the voice of the archangel, and with the trumpet call of God. And the dead in Christ will rise first. Then we who are alive and remain shall be caught up together with them in the clouds to meet the Lord in the air. And so we shall be forever with the Lord.
—1 THESSALONIANS 4:16

Amen, so be it!

CONTENTS

INTRODUCTION

HAVE YOU EVER GRAPPLED WITH THE DAUNTING question: "Are we living in the end, and are there signs given in God's Word and in the heavens as direct indicators of Earth's final days?" As we see catastrophes and calamities around the world and the continual upheaval of the foundations and values we hold sacred, one cannot help but wonder what the living God is saying to His church in this hour.

Proverbs 22:28 says, "Do not remove the ancient landmark which your fathers have set."

The land of Canaan was apportioned into twelve sections according to the size of each tribe. The boundaries of each allotment were described and carefully observed by the inhabitants. Land in each of the portions was divided by families, and everyone obtained a share in what God provided. Tampering with the boundaries was a serious offense, since the division of the land was ordained by God Himself.

Not all of the boundaries God intends for us to observe can be outlined on a topographical map, road atlas, or Google Earth. The Creator has also outlined the limits within which He expects us to live and prosper. Moving the fences God has already established leads to serious consequences.

We need not be unaware of where the lines of right living and godly behavior have been erected. God has given us signs in the heavens, celestial clues, as well as those articulated in His eternal Word to guide and protect us. Unfortunately, we live in a culture that has made a common practice of ignoring and overthrowing time-tested principles that would lead us to virtue and victory if we would but observe them. As a result, we find ourselves in territory that exposes us to hazards previously unknown.

Many years ago God spoke to me about proclaiming messages that were disappearing from the modern church. He instructed me to never neglect preaching about the reality of eternity, the certainty of heaven and hell, the rapture of the church, the second coming of the Lord, and especially sin and its terrible toll on humanity.

As I stood by these cultural cornerstones and cried out to those who were carelessly crossing the boundaries into uncharted and dangerous ground, I found that I was the exception rather than the rule. Trespassing onto other territory became not only acceptable but also fashionable. More and more people forsook the certainty and safety of a God-given inheritance for the folly of forbidden places. The fruit of rebellion seems sweet when first tasted, but afterward it becomes a mouth full of gravel (Proverbs 20:17).

I've declared it for years and am convinced more strongly than ever—it's time to return to the discarded values of the past! I'm so grateful to our Father God for His unspeakable gift of Jesus Christ, who paid the highest price and made the ultimate sacrifice to redeem each and every one of us to live victoriously in this life and to save us from the unfathomable suffering of an eternity without Him. And each day I look toward the heavens in anticipation of His soon return!

I'm also thankful for great men of God who made an indelible imprint upon my heart regarding these timeless truths as they preached them to me in my youth. As I think back, the first pastor I can remember from my childhood was a Freewill

Baptist evangelist, Andrew Workman—small in stature but towering in anointing, he admonished us to live right, according to God's Word and reminded us that Jesus was coming soon. I can still hear his words ringing in my ears, "If someone would just unlace my shoes, I could be raptured right now!" I pray for that same passion to be ignited in the hearts of preachers of the gospel today.

I sometimes marvel at the state of affairs in today's society—to think how far we have strayed in just one generation. You need not look any further than the headlines on any given day to see how far men have sunk into degradation and unholy lifestyles that are placed on display by the media and perpetuated by anyone who wants to have an opinion on the subject in the realm of social media. But the Bible reminds us to discern the times, and I believe the return of the Lord Jesus Christ is imminent!

I pray that you will discover on your journey through the pages of this book that God created signs in the heavens and made appointed seasons and set times on the fourth day of creation in order for us to be aware of His celestial time frame. How should we interpret the turmoil we see around us and in the world? Is there a message the Holy One of Israel wants to relay by the four red blood moons that appeared on the feasts of Passover and Tabernacles in 2014 and 2015? As you delve into the prophetic meaning of these signs, remember to keep your head up for your salvation is near, and the culmination of creation may indeed be closer than you have imagined!

Even those who are ignorant or misinformed regarding His Word can see celestial clues provided by a generous and gracious God through which we can discover His everlasting plan. Signs in the heavens send an unmistakable message of His plan, power, and purpose. Times and seasons that were established among the ancient Israelites for millennia are not obsolete religious observances, but designed specifically to help us know Him, His works, His ways, and how to navigate the times in which we live. All of these things point to a God-ordained conclusion to this age that is as steadfast and immovable as an ancient boundary marker telling us where our true and eternal home really is.

PART ONE

GOD'S
INVITATION
TO YOU

Chapter 1

UNDERSTANDING GOD'S TIMING

There are no two hours alike. Every hour is unique and the only one given at the moment, exclusive and endlessly precious. Judaism teaches us to be attached to holiness in time, to learn how to consecrate sanctuaries that emerge from the magnificent stream of a year.[1]

RABBI ABRAHAM JOSHUA HESCHEL

OUR GOD IS THE SOVEREIGN RULER OF THE UNIVERSE. HIS power is absolute, boundless, unrestricted, and supreme. His sovereignty over all of the activities of our beautiful world means that every detail of life as He created it is significant and able to give discernment to our eyes and direction to our hearts. How marvelous!

From the very creation of the world, God set in motion His times, cycles, and seasons. In the Bible I am using as I write these words, there are nearly 1,166 pages. Surprisingly, there are more than 800 verses in that Bible in which God declares He is concerned with times, seasons, and cycles. That's almost one verse for every page! We see this in His majestic creation narrative found in the opening paragraphs of the Book of Genesis:

> And God said, "Let there be lights in the expanse of the heavens to separate the day from the night, and let them be signs to indicate seasons, and days, and years. Let them be lights in the expanse of the heavens to give light on the earth." And it was so.
>
> —GENESIS 1:14–15

It is here that we get our first glimpse of day and night, of the seasons and years, and the lights in the heavens. When I first read these verses, I understood them to be a description of the beginning of all we see in the sky. But over time, as I read these verses again and again, greater insight into their deeper meaning began to emerge.

And then there came a moment, an epiphany, when I began to comprehend that these words were given to us to introduce the times and seasons by which God rules the world He created for mankind. Suddenly I understood that God isn't giving us astronomical information to enhance our stargazing; God is giving us a powerful revelation of how the heavenly bodies define His holy seasons and festivals and reveal His glory, if we will observe them.

In the original Hebrew, the Bible does not just say that the sun, moon, and stars will be for "signs"—at least not in the simple sense that this English word conveys. Instead, the original Hebrew says that the sun, moon, and stars are to mark "religious festivals" or "sacred times." They are tokens or signs of God's covenants and His sovereign, benevolent care for His people.

The Hebrew word behind this truth is *mo'edim* (moh-eh-DEEM). Usually it is translated "festivals," but it means so much more. This deeper revelation is vitally important to all that we are going to consider in this book. This word *mo'edim* means "a set or appointed time." It also means "appointed place, appointed meeting."[2] It indicates to "signify" or "act as a sign."

God has a sacred calendar, and He wants us to use it as He has commanded in Scripture because there is revelation in keeping the calendar of God. In fact, this is one of the great biblical secrets! When we keep the calendar of God, we will receive His truths, experience His presence, and be able to serve His purposes. The Hebrew translation of the word *festivals* as "appointed places" or "appointed meetings" reveals that God intends for us to use the heavenly bodies to mark out divine encounters.

God's calendar is so pregnant with meaning that one wise rabbi, the famous Rabbi Hirsch, said many years ago, "Catechism of the Jew is his calendar."[3] This isn't just true for Jews though. It is true for all of us who serve the living God. God has so coded truth into His set times, seasons, and festivals that those who understand them receive their truths and are irreversibly changed by them.

GOD'S SACRED CALENDAR

Most of us have lived our whole lives according to a solar calendar that is 365 days long, not knowing that God has a sacred calendar that is so much better. To understand God's sacred calendar, we must first realize that His calendar is based on a lunar (moon) cycle, not on a solar (sun) cycle. If you'll begin calling the calendar you use the Babylonian calendar, it will help you remember that this calendar is far removed from the one that God originally intended.

Our solar calendar begins on January 1, ends on December 31, and is divided into four seasons. It is made up of twelve months of approximately thirty days. Many of the months are named for ancient gods like January after the god Janus (Roman god of beginnings), February named for the god Februa (Roman festival of ritual purification), or March named for Mars (the ancient god of war). God's lunar calendar is quite different from the solar calendar.

If the first great truth of God's calendar is that it is a lunar calendar, then the second marvelous revelation is that God's calendar uses months that are much different from those to which we have become accustomed. God's lunar calendar is His will and His way. When we understand this, we can begin to number our days aright. Yet there are also practical reasons for using a lunar calendar. Because the moon changes every night, it marks the progress of time much more efficiently, and is far better for building a calendar upon than the sun.

If you spend time in the woods, forests, fields, lakes, and rivers, you know that animals actually change their feeding times every day based on the cycle of the moon, not the sun.

Farmers have been governing planting and harvesting by lunar cycles for centuries, using only the naked eye. Even the simplest farmer in the most rural setting can tell the stages of the moon just by looking in the night sky. All of nature is in harmony with the moon.

ENCOUNTERING HIS HOLY PRESENCE

As we begin to recognize God's lunar calendar in the Scriptures, we see that He has set specific times for us to encounter His holy presence and to discover and rediscover His plan and purpose for us.

What you have on your cell phone or in your date book is commonly referred to as the Gregorian calendar, or the Babylonian calendar. God date stamps events in the pages of Scripture by using the names of months from His calendar that are foreign to those of us who are only used to the solar or Gregorian calendar.

Let's look at a few Bible verses that illustrate this:

In the fourth year, in the month *Ziv* [zeev], the foundation of the house of the LORD was laid.

—1 KINGS 6:37, emphasis added

And in the eleventh year, in the month *Bul* [bool] (which is the eighth month), the house was completely finished. All the details and plans were met. So he took seven years to build it.

—1 KINGS 6:38, emphasis added

All the men of Israel assembled themselves before King Solomon at the feast in the month *Ethanim* [eth-ah-NEEM], which is the seventh month.

—1 KINGS 8:2, emphasis added

This temple was finished on the third day of the month *Adar* [uh-DAHR] during the sixth year of the reign of Darius the king.

—EZRA 6:15, emphasis added

The words of Nehemiah the son of Hakaliah. In the month *Kislev* [KEES-lev], in the twentieth year, while I was in Susa the palace...

—NEHEMIAH 1:1, emphasis added

In the month of *Nisan* [NEE-sahn], during the twentieth year of King Artaxerxes, when wine was before him, I took the wine and gave it to the king.

—NEHEMIAH 2:1, emphasis added

From these and many other Scriptures, it seems obvious that God wants us to use His calendar so that we can understand the times and seasons He defines in the pages of the Bible for divine encounters.

But there is more. Notice that God does not date events using the name of a month. Instead, He uses a number that corresponds to the month in His lunar calendar, also called the Hebrew calendar. Here are some examples:

> Speak to the children of Israel, saying: The fifteenth day of this *seventh month* shall be the Feast of Tabernacles for seven days to the LORD.
>
> —LEVITICUS 23:34, emphasis added

> The LORD spoke to Moses in the Wilderness of Sinai in the tent of meeting on the first day of the *second month* in the second year after they went out from the land of Egypt.
>
> —NUMBERS 1:1, emphasis added

> The fourteenth day of the *second month* at evening they will keep it.
>
> —NUMBERS 9:11, emphasis added

> On the fourteenth day of the *first month* is the Passover of the LORD.
>
> —NUMBERS 28:16, emphasis added

> You will have a holy assembly on the tenth day of this *seventh month*, and you will afflict yourselves.
>
> —NUMBERS 29:7, emphasis added

Each one of these months on God's lunar calendar are times and specific events for us to encounter God's holy presence so that we can more fully realize His amazing plan and purpose for our lives.

FOR THE SAKE OF WORSHIP

As we study God's end-time calendar together, I'll be throwing so many new ideas and terms at you that you might feel as though you've landed in a foreign country—and you have! You have landed in the foreign country of God's celebrations, cycles, set times, and seasons.

Even though it feels foreign, this is actually your native country, where you belong, if you have surrendered your life to the living God by accepting Jesus Christ as Messiah, Lord, and Savior. Some of our churches may have forgotten it, and we may have lost the revelation of it, but it's ours. This "land" is where we are called to dwell.

Get ready, because great things are about to be released into your life as you walk in a fresh revelation from and of God Almighty!

Let's begin this journey of discovery and revelation together by looking at the differences between the lunar calendar and the solar calendar. The following chart lists the months of the lunar calendar, along with their approximate times in the Gregorian or solar calendar.

Notice that the beginning, end, and seasons of God's year do not correspond to the beginning, end, and seasons of the solar year. The beginning of God's year is not January 1, the birthday of His Son is not December 25, and Resurrection Day is not Easter. There is a reason for the way God constructed His lunar calendar, which we'll talk about in a minute.

For now, though, let's take a look at the months of God in order and in their approximate setting in the solar calendar we use now, keeping the following three simple things in mind: 1) God's calendar is a lunar calendar, not the solar calendar we are accustomed to; 2) God's calendar is comprised of months different from those in our solar calendar; and 3) God's year is different from the year we are familiar with. God is going to position you using these three truths, so remember them.

	Name of Month	Occurrence in Solar Calendar
1.	Nisan (NEE-sahn)	March–April
2.	Iyar (EE-yahr)—called Ziv (zeev) in 1 Kings 6:1, 37	April–May
3.	Sivan (see-VAHN)	May–June
4.	Tammuz (tam-MOOZ)	June–July
5.	Av (ahv)	July–August
6.	Elul (el-OOL)	August–September
7.	Tishrei (tish-RAY)—called Ethanim (ETH-uh-neem) in 1 Kings 8:2	September–October
8.	Cheshvan (KESH-vahn)—called Bul (bool) in 1 Kings 6:38	October–November
9.	Kislev (KEES-lev)	November–December
10.	Tevet (teh-VEHT)	December–January
11.	Shevat (shuh-VAHT)	January–February
12.	Adar I (uh-DAHR)	February–March
12b.	Adar Beit (uh-DAHR bait)	Leap Years

Now, let's look at a fourth profound truth about God's calendar: *God's calendar is designed for the sake of worship and divine encounters.* It is defined by His appointed feasts and His declared, sacred seasons that He calls us to celebrate. God reveals His nature and His character to us through His times, cycles, and seasons. The fact that God's calendar is dotted with festivals and holy days is a revelation in itself.

Think of God's calendar much like a sacred alarm clock that reminds us to arise and remember His great deeds, to celebrate His abundant goodness, and to worship Him for His glorious acts yet to come! How exciting!

This fourth truth is the key to understanding the whole of the Bible, particularly the meaning of the life of Jesus Christ on Earth. When we come to understand the earthly life of Jesus in light of these festivals, the truth of who He is explodes into our lives. There is so much revelation waiting for us in the calendar of God.

INTIMACY WITH GOD THROUGH REVELATION AND CELEBRATION

Before we go any further I want to address a possible misunderstanding. Am I trying to drag us back under the law by urging that we know and celebrate the sacred seasons of God? Absolutely, positively, unequivocally not!

My goal is revelation and celebration, not legalism. My desire is for us to obey God and to see Him in the greater revelation that is available through His *mo'edim*—His signs and festivals. My deeper ambition is intimacy with God.

Understanding God's times and seasons is like a husband gaining insight into a wife so he can more fully love her, care for her, and protect her. This is exactly what God desires for us in our relationship with Him. He desires for us to draw closer to Him and learn to walk in His ways. This is His primary ambition. We have a choice: focus only on the rules and the requirements, or look deeper and perceive the "language" of God through the law and the revelation of the One who gave the requirements.

Everything that God has designed for us is an invitation to intimacy with Him. Take for instance, the kosher laws. Observing kosher is a hallmark of Jewish identity, yet some would look at kosher laws and see only "do not taste; do not touch"—the arcane requirements and regulations of a restrictive God to force obedience with judgment and condemnation. Nothing could be further from God's heart.

The deeper truth of kosher laws may well be that in the smallest and most mundane matters of life—something as simple as eating—we welcome God and acknowledge Him as the sustainer of life. For Jews, life is a sacred endeavor, and holiness an appropriate response to even the most ordinary of everyday activities. By observing kosher, Jewish people illustrate that we are not animals to eat what we please, when we please, and how we please.

Through kosher laws, Jewish children learn patience, order, obedience, thankfulness, discipline, manners, and a revelation of God as provider and sustainer of their sustenance. While there is a physical benefit of kosher laws, they serve as a call to pause, reflect, and acknowledge God.

Again, I am not advocating that we come back under the Law. Jesus said He did not come to abolish the Law but to fulfill it. My heart's desire is that, by God's grace, we can recover the new covenant purpose of much of God's old covenant requirements, because that's what those of us who are in Christ are meant to do.

As one of the early church fathers said, "In the Old Testament the New Testament is concealed; in the New Testament the Old Testament is revealed."[4] My heart's prayer is for us to receive the fullest revelation of God our Father through Jesus Christ by the power of the Holy Spirit.

JEWISH NEW YEARS?

It should come as no surprise by now to know that God looks at things differently from the way men do. After all, He has a different perspective from His vantage point beyond the limitations of time and space. The ideas of time and space were created by God to enable His ultimate creation, man, to flourish and be fulfilled in a world God created especially for him.

As I mentioned earlier, God's way of measuring time from the fourth day of creation focused on the moon, which is a different way of perceiving time than the calendar that most of us in the Western world use, which is based on the sun.

God's appointed festivals always occur on the same day of the same month in the Jewish calendar, but those of us depending on the solar calendar wonder why Jewish holidays are in one month in a specific year and a different month in another year. Since the Jewish calendar is based on a lunar cycle that lasts 29.5 days, there are any number of discrepancies between God's appointed seasons and our more familiar calendar months.

However, since a month cannot include a half day, months on the Jewish calendar are either twenty-nine or thirty days. Lest you think this is confusing, just consider how difficult it is for most people to remember how many days are in a particular Gregorian month. It may be thirty, thirty-one, twenty-eight, or in leap years, twenty-nine.

When God gave Moses instructions for the Passover festival in Exodus 12, He specified that the month, or new moon, would be the first month of the year. The people of Israel were about to experience a rebirth as a result of their miraculous deliverance from their Egyptian taskmasters. They had new lives because of God's intervention, so it makes sense that they should consider this period of time the beginning of their year.

However, this understanding causes confusion when we see later that Rosh Hashanah (rahsh hah-SHAH-nah), or the head of the year, is celebrated in the seventh month. Which is correct?

The short answer is that both are. Let me explain it this way. The first month, or Nisan, is the beginning of the sacred or ceremonial year and begins with the festival of Passover, which commemorates Israel's deliverance from Egypt. As we know from the biblical record, this was also the time that God chose to bring about the ultimate freedom from the bondage of sin, which culminated in the death, burial, and resurrection of Jesus.

The seventh month, or Tishrei, is the beginning of the civil year. It is the date from which years are counted for the purposes of Sabbath years and Jubilee years. It is also traditionally regarded as the date that began recorded history, which included the creation of Adam and Eve.

This discrepancy isn't so strange when we consider that many nations have different beginnings of years for different reasons. Many Western nations celebrate the beginning of a new year on January 1. This occasion involves revelry as well as a renewed determination to set goals, make resolutions, and manage affairs differently in the days to come.

However, for business and economic purposes, governments and many corporations operate according to a fiscal year, which has entirely different beginning and ending dates. In addition, every parent of a school-age child is familiar with a school year, which usually begins in the fall and ends in the spring. You may actually celebrate more than one beginning of a new year without realizing that you're doing it.

It's thrilling to unlock these truths and understand God's divine purpose for our lives in the calendar He has ordained for us to observe!

Chapter 2

THE PATTERN OF
GOD'S CALENDAR

*It is He who changes the times and the seasons; He
removes kings and sets up kings; He gives wisdom to the
wise and knowledge to those who know understanding.*

DANIEL 2:21

THE HEBREW CALENDAR IS INGENIOUSLY SYMBOLIC AND
prophetically accurate. We are going to examine its two
seasons—the spring and fall feasts—as we learn more about the
powerful drama that birthed the Jewish nation.

We'll begin our study with a brief overview—a "fly-over," if you
will—so that you can get the pattern of God's festivals clearly
embedded in your heart. We will examine each of the festivals in
these two seasons in greater detail in subsequent chapters.

The best place to start is always at the beginning, which in the
Hebrew calendar is not January in winter, but much more appropriately in the month of Nisan, the first month in the Hebrew
calendar.

The month of Nisan occurs in spring (March–April), a time
of new life and rebirth and a time of deliverance for the Jewish
people. It is in the month of Nisan that God Almighty performed

the miracle of delivering Israel out of Egyptian bondage and slavery, giving birth to the nation of Israel. It is in this season of spring deliverance that we find the Passover, the first of the spring feasts.

THE SPRING FEASTS—
DELIVERANCE

Passover (Pesach)—a celebration of freedom

> In each generation every individual is obliged to feel as though he or she personally came out of Egypt.... Therefore we are obliged to thank, praise, laud, glorify, and exalt, to honor, bless, extol and adore Him who performed all these wonders for our ancestors and for us: He brought us out of slavery into freedom, out of sorrow into joy, out of mourning into a holiday, out of darkness into daylight and out of bondage into redemption. Let us then sing before Him a new song: Halleluyah![1]
>
> —THE PASSOVER HAGGADAH

According to God's command, Passover always begins on the fourteenth of Nisan. In Leviticus 23:5 the Lord told Moses, "On the fourteenth day of the first month at evening is the LORD's Passover." On this night, all the people of Israel reenact the first Passover, which occurred in Egypt when God delivered His people from their 430 years of Egyptian bondage.

In order to fully understand the life of Jesus Christ on Earth, and what the Apostle Paul was teaching about the Lord Jesus, we must understand the power of the Passover. Passover is one of the most significant feasts celebrated by the Jewish people. It is a key to the full revelation of the sacrifice of our Savior, the Passover Lamb of God. The Feast of Passover is mentioned many times in the New Testament.[2]

God's people, the Israelites, came to Egypt to escape drought in their homeland. Once in Egypt, they prospered and multiplied to such an extent that Pharaoh began to fear them, and so he enslaved them. In the midst of their slavery and oppression, the people of God cried out to Yahweh to save them. God heard their prayers and answered them by inflicting a series of ten plagues on the Egyptians. Each plague demonstrated God's power, yet Pharaoh's heart remained hardened toward the Israelites until the tenth and last plague, the death of the firstborn sons.

Before God swept through Egypt killing all of the firstborn males, He instructed Moses to have all the Israelites mark their doorposts with the blood of a sacrificial lamb. In this way, when the Lord came and saw the sacrifice, He would pass over their house, sparing their firstborn baby boy. This is the origin of the Jewish celebration of Passover. Exodus 12:14 says: "This day shall be a memorial to you, and you shall keep it as a feast to the Lord. Throughout your generations you shall keep it a feast by an eternal ordinance."

The Lord gave Moses instructions for celebrating the Passover. He told him to tell the people to eat lamb with bitter herbs and unleavened bread. They were to eat it all in haste with their shoes on, their robes tucked in their belts, and their staffs in their hands. In other words, they were to remember the urgency of that first night and be prepared to leave at once.

Since the day of their amazing deliverance, the people of God have celebrated Passover. It is a pilgrimage feast of Israel, which means it is one of the three feasts that God commanded all male Israelites to celebrate each year in Jerusalem.

The Feast of Unleavened Bread (Chag HaMatzot) (khahg hah-maht-ZOHT)—sanctification

The second spring feast of Israel is the Feast of Unleavened Bread. This feast commemorates the events that immediately followed the first Passover in Egypt. The Feast of Unleavened Bread is important to God because it was "on this very day I brought your armies out of the land of Egypt" (Exodus 12:17).

When God told His people to slaughter a lamb and to place its blood upon their doorposts so the curse of death would pass over them, He also made the declaration: "Seven days you shall eat unleavened bread. On the first day you shall put away leaven out of your houses, for whoever eats leavened bread from the first day until the seventh day, that person shall be cut off from Israel" (Exodus 12:15).

Each year in spring, by the fifteenth of Nisan, the day following Passover, the Jewish people have already removed all yeast from their houses, because yeast is symbolic of sin. During the feast they eat only unleavened bread, just as their ancestors did when God delivered them from Egypt.

The Feast of Unleavened Bread is a thrilling, weeklong celebration. We'll get into the details of this feast later, but it is exciting already to see that holiness and deliverance are linked together in this second of the seven feasts of Israel.

Firstfruits (Reishit Katzir) (reh-SHEET kaht-ZEER)— resurrection of the church

The third spring feast of Israel is the Feast of Firstfruits. It is a celebration of the goodness of the land that God gave to His people after their wilderness wanderings, and is celebrated on the first Sunday after Passover, during the Feast of Unleavened Bread. In Leviticus 23:10–11 God decreed,

> Speak to the children of Israel, and say to them: "When you come into the land which I give to you, and reap its harvest, then you shall bring a sheaf of the firstfruits of your harvest to the priest. He shall wave the sheaf before the LORD, to be

accepted on your behalf; on the day after the Sabbath the priest shall wave it."

—NKJV

This feast may appear on the surface to be less important than the other spring feasts, but let me assure you that for the New Testament believer, the Feast of Firstfruits is one of the most significant and critical of all. Hint: the Jewish people celebrate Firstfruits on the same day Jesus, the ultimate Firstfruit, was resurrected.

Pentecost (Shavu'ot)—the summer harvest

Pentecost occurs fifty days after Firstfruits, according to Leviticus 23:15–16. For the Jewish people, Pentecost is one of God's set times, representing His summer harvest, and acknowledging the magnificent yield He provided for His people by His mighty hand. It is the second of the pilgrimage feasts of Israel. Here is how God commanded His people to observe this feast:

> From the day after the Sabbath, the day you brought the sheaf of the wave offering, count off seven full weeks. Count off fifty days up to the day after the seventh Sabbath, and then present an offering of new grain to the LORD.
>
> From wherever you live, bring two loaves made of two-tenths of an ephah [EE-fah] of the finest flour, baked with yeast, as a wave offering of firstfruits to the LORD.
>
> Present with this bread seven male lambs, each a year old and without defect, one young bull and two rams. They will be a burnt offering to the LORD, together with their grain offerings and drink offerings—a food offering, an aroma pleasing to the LORD.
>
> Then sacrifice one male goat for a sin offering and two lambs, each a year old, for a fellowship offering. The priest is to wave the two lambs before the LORD as a wave offering,

together with the bread of the firstfruits. They are a sacred offering to the LORD for the priest. On that same day you are to proclaim a sacred assembly and do no regular work. This is to be a lasting ordinance for the generations to come, wherever you live."

—LEVITICUS 23:15–21, NIV

For the Israelites, Pentecost was a celebration of ingathering. In the Old Testament it is sometimes called the Feast of Harvest and the Feast of Weeks. Passover ended with Pentecost, with the harvesting of wheat, which was the last of the grains to ripen.

The Jewish celebration of Pentecost also contains elements that seem to signify a greater reach than was represented in the pure celebrations of Passover. Only leavened bread is used in this Feast of Weeks, perhaps signifying that God had the Gentile world in mind, which were represented by "unclean" leaven. That would be perfectly in keeping with what took place on this day centuries later.

There was no other day with more prophetic significance for such an outpouring than Pentecost—the day of the Feast of Ingathering, which had been decreed hundreds of years earlier by God Almighty Himself!

For the Christian church, Pentecost has the symbolic theme of the ingathering of the Gentile world. According to Acts 2, the Holy Spirit fell on 120 people in a house in Jerusalem on the Day of Pentecost, pouring out upon believers, equipping and empowering them to be witnesses. Filled and empowered by God's Spirit, they were to go and gather the human harvest of God from the far-flung corners of the earth, not just from the nation of Israel. We know that when the Holy Spirit was poured out upon the early church on the Day of Pentecost, many nations were immediately impacted.

These spring feasts of God—Passover, the Feast of Unleavened

Bread, the Feast of Firstfruits, and Pentecost—are divinely declared celebrations to commemorate the great deliverance from bondage in Egypt, purity among God's people, the richness of the Promised Land, and the calling of God's people to reach the nations of the earth. As we study these feasts in greater detail in the coming chapters, you will begin to clearly see how God has brought them to His fullness in His magnificent Son, Jesus Christ.

THE FALL FEASTS—REPENTANCE

The fall feasts of God begin in the seventh month of the Hebrew calendar, many months after Pentecost. The closeness of Passover and Pentecost and the fact that a great deal of time separates them from the fall feasts are very symbolic and prophetic, as we will discover. That these later feasts begin in the seventh month gives us some indication about their theme and message. They celebrate completion, with judgment and new beginnings.

Rosh Hashanah—the Feast of Trumpets (Yom Teru'ah)—Jewish New Year

> On Rosh Hashanah all human beings pass before Him as troops, as it is said, "the Lord looks down from heaven, He sees all mankind. From His dwelling place He gazes on all the inhabitants of the earth, He who fashions the hearts of them all, who discerns all their doings."[3]
> —RABBI DR. REUVEN HAMMER

Rosh Hashanah, also known as the Feast of Trumpets, the first of the fall festivals, begins on the first day of the seventh month of Tishrei. The Lord had told Moses,

> Speak to the children of Israel, saying: In the seventh month,
> on the first day of the month, you shall have a sabbath, a
> memorial with the blowing of trumpets, a holy convocation.
> —LEVITICUS 23:24

The "trumpet" that the Jewish people blow is known as the *shofar* (show-FAHR), and it is often God's instrument of choice. The shofar has many purposes, but at the beginning of the fall feasts, it was employed as both a wake-up call for the people of God and a summons to repentance.

Rosh Hashanah is the Jewish New Year's Day. Its urgent call to consecration was necessary because the Feast of Trumpets came ten days before the holiest day of the Hebrew year, the Day of Atonement. During these ten days of self-examination, the people of Israel were to repent of their sins and make right any wrongs they could before they reached the Day of Atonement, or Yom Kippur (yohm kee-POOR), a day of judgment for God's people.

The Day of Atonement (Yom Kippur)—Israel's national salvation

> On Yom Kippur, the ritual trial reaches its conclusion. The
> people finally drop all their defenses and excuses and throw
> themselves on the mercy of the court, yet the same people
> never lose the conviction that they will be pardoned. This
> atonement is by divine grace; it is above and beyond the indi-
> vidual effort or merit.[4]
> —RABBI IRVING GREENBERG

> Yom Kippur is the idea that we get a second chance before
> God forgives us for the mistakes that we've made. And we all
> get a second chance in life.[5]
> —RABBI SHMUEL HERZFELD

The most significant and high holy day of the entire Jewish year is Yom Kippur, the Day of Atonement. God Almighty spoke this decree directly to Moses:

> Also on the tenth day of this seventh month there shall be the Day of Atonement. It shall be a holy convocation to you, and you shall humble yourselves, and offer a food offering made by fire to the LORD.
> —LEVITICUS 23:27

Yom Kippur is a fearsome and weighty day, reserved for self-examination and deep introspection, the day the people of Israel are most aware of their personal and national sins.

On this day, in Old Testament times, the high priest was permitted to enter the holy of holies, the singular place of the most tangible presence of the Almighty on planet Earth. Here, he would call upon the name of God, offering blood sacrifices for the sins of the Jewish people.

It was the most solemn of occasions, and the people were forbidden to do any work. God, the Lord on High, judged all things on the Day of Atonement. Wrongs were grieved, destinies were decided, and judgments were handed down.

Yom Kippur marks the end of the Days of Awe, a ten-day period of repentance and retrospect.

The Feast of Tabernacles (Sukkot)—a picture of the millennial kingdom

The Feast of Tabernacles, also known as Sukkot or Booths, is the seventh and final feast, and concludes the year on the Hebrew calendar. It is also the third of the pilgrimage feasts. The Feast of Tabernacles commences on the fifteenth day of the seventh month, at a set time, and continues for seven days. The proliferation of sevens in this feast—the seventh feast, that takes place in the seventh month, and lasts seven days—is prophetic evidence that this feast was of the highest priority to God, since seven is the number associated with God's divine completion and perfection in the Bible.

The purpose of the Feast of Tabernacles was to remember how God, by supernatural and miraculous means, provided for the Israelites in the wilderness. Here is His divine decree:

> You shall dwell in booths for seven days. All who are native children of Israel shall dwell in booths, that your generations may know that I made the children of Israel dwell in booths when I brought them out of the land of Egypt: I am the LORD your God.
> —LEVITICUS 23:42–43

God's instruction is implicit here: the Israelites were to live in crude booths during the Feast of Tabernacles as a way to remember God's provision for them as they wandered through the treacherous wilderness for forty years, before entering the Promised Land.

Yet, there is another, more universal purpose of this seventh and final feast. It is the single feast that is mentioned in Scripture as eventually being required of all nations if they are to come under the blessing of God.

We will examine the symbolism of the Feast of Tabernacles more fully in the chapters to come, but for now it is important to realize that the seventh feast of God, taking place in the seventh month, and eventually being required for all nations, is a direct indication of the prophetic power and profound importance of this set time of celebration.

CONCLUSION

Much of what we've covered in this brief "fly-over" of the seven major feasts of God from the Hebrew calendar may be new to you. These festivals are the *mo'edim*, the sacred signs of God for all of His people. As we study God's divine calendar and His truths as they are symbolized and revealed in these feasts, let us begin to master these patterns of God and embrace His truths.

These "big seven" are God's original seven feasts as found in Scripture. The Jewish people today celebrate two other feasts. One is Hanukkah (hahn-ah-KUH), a celebration of the rededication of the temple by the Maccabees around 165 BC. The other is Purim (poo-REEM), a celebration of the events described in the Book of Esther. Both are important, and we will examine the powerful symbolism of Purim later, but for now, we must be careful not to confuse them with God's original seven feasts in Scripture.

Chapter 3

RED BLOOD MOONS— BLIGHT OR BLESSING?

I believe we are living in the time of Elul, and God is calling us to repentance. The trumpet is about to sound, signifying our Messiah's return. Those who are living for Him long for this day and will see it as a wonderful time of joy and triumph. But those who do not turn to God will experience terror and destruction.[1]

RABBI JONATHAN BERNIS

When Jews appear for Divine judgment, the angels say to them: "Don't be afraid, the Judge…is your Father."[2]

MIDRASH TEHILLIM

WHEN I TAKE IN THE GLORY OF OUR CREATOR'S HANDI-work in the endless night sky, I am amazed by what I see. I know I am witnessing what God set in motion before the foundations of the earth were established. God was speaking the twinkle of cosmic entities into existence before your mother ever saw the twinkle in your father's eye.

Science reveals that what we see in the evening skies has been traveling for light-years to arrive at a point where our naked eye can see it. It is not as though an angelic being in the heavens turned on a lamp at the very moment you began looking upward! Those lights have been in transit, sometimes for centuries.

I want to encourage you to undertake a special task before you begin this chapter—a homework assignment, if you will. Whether your home is on the banks of the Jordan River or deep in the hills of West Virginia, I want you to take a moment to observe the grand and glorious fourth day of creation. Yes, that's right, the "fourth day" of creation.

Our heavenly Father formed the sun to bring us light and warmth by day and the moon to illuminate the night for us. Yet no words of mine can compare to what the Bible declares regarding this fourth-day miracle. Genesis 1:14–19 says it most beautifully:

> God said, "Let there be lights in the expanse of the heavens to separate the day from the night, and let them be signs to indicate seasons, and days, and years. Let them be lights in the expanse of the heavens to give light on the earth." And it was so. God made two great lights: the greater light to rule the day and the lesser light to rule the night. He made the stars also. Then God set them in the expanse of the heavens to give light on the earth, to rule over the day and over the night, and to divide the light from the darkness. Then God saw that it was good. So the evening and the morning were the fourth day.

Stop for a moment, right now if you can, and walk outside, look up at the vast expanse above, and thank our heavenly Father for creating light by day and by night. Then ask yourself, when was the last time you watched the sun set or the moon rise? If you can carve out only a few minutes to watch the dusty red horizon cloak itself in a cover of moonlit darkness, you will see the heavens open up like a rose in spring bloom, unfolding illuminations, as each star twinkles into view. It's magnificent!

Whenever I have the opportunity to stop and drink in these celestial lights, I am overwhelmed by God's magnitude. I feel like David must have felt when he wrote Psalm 19:1, 4:

> The heavens declare the glory of God, and the firmament shows His handiwork.... Their line has gone out through all the earth and their words to the end of the world.

As I contemplate all of this I realize that what really fascinates me isn't the creation. It is the Creator of the universe and His heavenly splendor that fill me with awe-struck wonder.

Think about it: the sky that glowed so gloriously on the evening you were married or the night your child was born—everything that caused that sky to exist on those important days was set in motion on the fourth day of creation. Our all-knowing, all-powerful God put His divine machinery in motion so that the sky above you would appear in the exact arrangement you saw on that particular day.

Why am I sharing all of this with you right now? Because it is foundational to what I'm about to unveil regarding the phenomenon of the Red Blood Moons. If we don't keep these foundational truths about all that God set in motion on the fourth day of creation in mind, we could easily become caught up in, and even swept away by, all of the apocalyptic rhetoric surrounding the Red Blood Moons that is sweeping through our culture right now. We need to seek God's truths not sensational rhetoric.

Rather than allowing your attention to be drawn to the latest end-time theories or predictions, if you remember that everything you behold in the sky at any given moment was planned and set in motion by God on the fourth day of creation, then your attention will be on the real question, which is, "Why would God program His celestial bodies to bring these signs into view now? What is God telling us?" This is the real issue, the real question.

RED BLOOD MOONS

A Red Blood Moon (or some say Blood Red Moon) is a naturally occurring galactic phenomenon. But where did this name come from? Some say overexcited preachers gave this phenomenon its dramatic name, but that's not the case. NASA actually coined the name, which they borrowed from the ancient name for a "Hunter's Moon" or "Red Blood Moon," making it an official, modern term.[3] When you think about it, the name is appropriate because they are describing a moon that is blood red in color.

Remember, the moon has no light of its own; it only reflects a source of light that comes from beyond itself. The moon shows brightly in our night sky because it reflects the light of the sun.

We, the church, are not unlike the moon in that we have no "light," no power, and no glory of our own, because we are called and equipped to reflect those characteristics of our heavenly Father. But that is a topic for another book!

Occasionally we experience what is called a lunar eclipse, when the sun, moon, and earth align in such a way that the earth blocks the light from the sun that would normally shine on the moon. When this happens, the moon appears darkened and eerie in the night sky. Perhaps you've seen a lunar eclipse before, or you've seen some of the dramatic photographs of this phenomenon.

When the earth completely blocks the light from the sun, as the sun's light passes through earth's atmosphere and bends toward the moon, it makes the moon appear reddish in color. For some reason the earth's atmosphere filters the light of the sun, while blocking most of the other colors in the spectrum, permitting only red light to pass through and splash upon the moon. This creates the vivid and memorable sight of a Red Blood Moon.

These Red Blood Moons have occurred throughout history and continue today. They are somewhat rare, and we probably wouldn't be paying so much attention to them today if their only oddity were this matter of color.

What has brought Red Blood Moons into the headlines today is that at times—though very, very rarely—this phenomenon occurs in a series of four. The sophisticated word for this is *tetrad*. For purposes of our study, *tetrad* means "four in a row during a defined period of time." So, if a Red Blood Moon is rare, having four of them in a row almost never happens!

But the rarity of this phenomenon does not end there. Think about this: God placed the sun, moon, and stars in the heavens to delineate sacred seasons and ceremonies. Suppose we ask ourselves if these Red Blood Moon tetrads ever coincided with the Hebrew calendar and Jewish feasts in a way that signals their significance. What then?

As you recall, the Hebrew word *mo'edim,* often translated "feasts" or "festivals," actually means "signs" or "symbols." In light of this, our question now becomes, "Do these tetrads of Red Blood Moons signify anything to us?" Let's explore further.

We know that in Jewish tradition, the occurrence of Red Blood Moons has most often been taken as a sign of war. The Jewish people historically considered them bad omens, usually relating to bloodshed.

The Jewish Talmud (TAL-mood), the commentary of the ancient rabbis upon the Torah, declares, "When the moon is in eclipse, it is a bad omen for Israel. If its face is as red as blood, the sword is coming to the world."

In light of this, let's survey some of the times in history when a tetrad of Red Blood Moons coincided with important dates on the Hebrew calendar that signaled historic events on Earth.

1. The crucifixion of Jesus

A Red Blood Moon tetrad occurred during AD 32 and 33, the period when our Lord Jesus Christ was crucified on the angry, mean, biting beam of Calvary. These blood moons coincided with Passover and the Feast of Tabernacles in these years.[4]

2. Jewish persecution

Four total lunar eclipses occurred on Passover and the Feast of Tabernacles, in 161 and 163 BC, coinciding with the worst persecution of the Jewish people up to that time.[5]

3. Defeat of the Arabs

Four total lunar eclipses occurred on Passover and on Yom Kippur, in AD 795 and 796, when Charlemagne, emperor of the Holy Roman Empire, established a buffer between France and Spain, ending centuries of Arab incursion into Western Europe.[6]

4. Another defeat of the Arabs

Four total lunar eclipses occurred in 842–843, when Muslims from Africa attacked and looted Rome. Shortly after these eclipses, in 860–861, the Byzantine Empire defeated Arab armies at a great battle in what is now Turkey, and permanently stopped the Islamic infiltration of Eastern Europe.[7]

5. The expulsion of the Jews from Spain

Four total lunar eclipses occurred in 1493–1494, only months after King Ferdinand and Queen Isabella of Spain expelled the Jews from that nation, commissioned Christopher Columbus to sail to the New World, and ended the Spanish Inquisition.[8]

6. The Jewish War of Independence

In 1948, the United Nations voted in favor of statehood for the nation of Israel, and she took her place among the nations of the world. Israel was immediately forced to defend her newly gained independence against the surrounding Arab nations, a conflict that continues to this day. In the years that immediately followed Israeli independence, Red Blood Moons occurred according to this pattern on the Hebrew calendar:[9]

- Passover, April 13, 1949

- Feast of Tabernacles, October 7, 1949

- Passover, April 2, 1950

- Feast of Tabernacles, September 26, 1950

7. The Six-Day War

Though the 1967 war was in one sense, a continuation of the ongoing conflict between Israel and her Arab enemies, the war was particularly significant. As a result of this series of battles, Jerusalem was reunited with the Jewish people for the first time in nearly nineteen hundred years.

The story of this war is so replete with miracles that it reads like a page from the Bible. However equally miraculous is the fact that a tetrad of Red Blood Moons occurred at that time, and once again, they fell on Passover and the Feast of Tabernacles.[10] Specifically, they occurred on:

- Passover, April 24, 1967

- Feast of Tabernacles, October 18, 1967

- Passover, April 13, 1968

- Feast of Tabernacles, October 6, 1968

Do you see the pattern forming here? Not only do we have the rare reoccurrence of a tetrad of Red Blood Moons, but we also have the even more rare alignment of the Red Blood Moon phenomenon with God's holy days.

When we consider that this alignment also transpired on some of the most significant dates in Israel's history, it is too much to be merely a coincidence. We have to ask, "What is the Lord of history telling us? What is the meaning of these *mo'edim*? What are we meant to understand?"

I believe it is time for us to consider these celestial clues and mark them well. As I might say if I were preaching, "We're about to see a thing! Speak on, Holy Ghost!"

Remember, our God is a God of cycles and patterns, of times and seasons. If we are to understand what He is telling us, we must become historians, taught by the Holy Spirit and who consider the meaning of God's time stamps.

Let's take, for example, what the ninth day of the month of Av, the fifth month of the Jewish year, has to show us. On this single date, some of the worst events in the history of the Jewish people occurred:[11]

- In 1313 BC the children of Israel cried out to God and declared that they would rather go back to Egypt than enter the Promised Land (Numbers 14).

- In 423 BC the Babylonians destroyed the temple of God.

- In AD 70 the temple of God was again destroyed, this time by Roman armies.

- In AD 133 the famous Simon Bar Kochba rebellion of the Jews against Roman rule occurred.

- In 1095 Pope Urban II launched the first Crusade to the Holy Land.

- In 1290 King Edward I expelled the Jewish people from England.

- In 1492 King Ferdinand and Queen Isabella expelled the Jews from Spain.

- In 1914 World War I began. Historians consider World War II—with its Jewish ghettoes and concentration camps—the continuation of World War I.

Now, are you beginning to see how vitally important it is that we view time through the lens of God's calendar and His celestial clues? When we use God's calendar, considering His signs in the heavens, and understanding the spiritual battles that are taking place on the earth, we can receive tremendous revelation from our great and mighty God.

Special acknowledgement

I'd like to take this opportunity to thank Pastor Mark Biltz of El Shaddai Ministries who, to my knowledge, was the first person to bring the tremendous revelation of Red Blood Moons to our attention by his in-depth study on this subject. What a wonderful gift to the body of Christ! His research certainly sparked my interest in this topic, and what a great blessing it's been to me and so many others.

STAR OF BETHLEHEM

Just as we have experienced the phenomenon of the Red Blood Moons tetrad, it's of interest to note that there is a current series of planet rotations wherein Jupiter and Venus converge (called a conjunction), which is occurring four times between the years of

2014 and 2016. This particular series of conjunctions is very similar to the series of conjunctions that occurred between 3 and 2 BC, which came to be known as the Star of Bethlehem around the time of Jesus' birth.

The dates of these wondrous "Star of Bethlehem" occurrences are[12]:

- August 18, 2014

- June 30, 2015

- October 26, 2015

- August 27, 2016

I just love to brag on our Father God and the wondrous universe that He set in motion on the fourth day of creation!

THE FALL FEASTS—TROUBLED TIMES

Historians throughout the centuries have noted, somewhat in amazement, that the early fall months of any given year are frequently filled with deadly conflicts and epic events, as if the earth and its inhabitants are convulsing and contracting, rocking and reeling under some kind of supernatural power. Well, I believe that's exactly what happens, but the question is, "Why?"

These fall months are also the most financially troubled of all months. They are historically the worst months for the US Stock Exchange. The stock market collapse, known as the Great Depression, began during October 1929. The famous Black Monday, during which the market lost 22 percent of its value—the worst day of losses since the Great Depression—began on October 19, 1987. And, let's not forget that on September 17, 2001, just days after the disastrous events of September 11, the stock market lost 685 points in a single day.

Perhaps all this upheaval is the result of, and an indication of, the invisible spiritual war that rages against God's purposes on the earth. Perhaps the devil knows that great destinies are in play during the fall feasts of Israel, because they are designed and divinely directed to release overwhelming power to God's people at specific times on God's calendar. Whatever the reason, there is no question that fall is a troubled time.

Consider this: in August of 2014, American journalist James Foley was kidnapped by the Islamic State and beheaded. Then, in September 2014, Steven Sotloff, a Jew and an American journalist, was beheaded by the Islamic State, as was David Haines, a forty-four-year-old British humanitarian and engineer. Just a few weeks later, forty-four-year-old Peter Kassig, an aid worker in Syria and former US Ranger, met the same fate. There are countless other incidences just like the ones I've named, not to mention other disturbing events like the destructive volcano that erupted in Pahoa, Hawaii, in October 2014, and the Ebola outbreak in the same time frame that claimed thousands of lives. There are pages and pages of such troubling data from years past, confirming that the fall months, during the fall feasts of Israel, are markedly the most troubled times of the year.

But why is all this so important to us right now? It is important because we are already into the next tetrad of Red Blood Moons as I write these words. Thanks to NASA computers, I can tell you the exact dates:[13]

- First Day of Feast of Passover, April 15, 2014

- First Day of Feast of Tabernacles, October 8, 2014

- First Day of Feast of Passover, April 4, 2015

- First Day of Feast of Tabernacles, September 28, 2015

Now let's add yet another layer of alignment to our understanding of the Red Blood Moons in 2015. As you may recall, under the law of God, and in the economy of Israel, every fifty years is a Jubilee year. In a Jubilee year, all debts are forgiven, all slaves are freed, and the land is given rest.

Leviticus 25:8–9 says:

> Thou shalt number seven sabbaths of years unto thee, seven times seven years; and the space of the seven sabbaths of years shall be unto thee forty and nine years. Then shalt thou cause the trumpet of the jubilee to sound on the tenth day of the seventh month, in the day of atonement shall ye make the trumpet sound throughout all your land.
>
> —KJV

Additionally, every seventh year is also a Sabbath or sabbatical year. In Hebrew it is called a *Shemitah* (SHMIH-tah) year. In a Shemitah year the people rest, and the land is allowed to lie fallow.

Shemitah began on September 25, 2014, and will end on September 13, 2015, the same time frame in which a tetrad of Red Blood Moons coincides with the feasts of God. This means that 2015 concludes a Sabbath year—a Shemitah year—in which the people of God are meant to enter in a God-given rest. This also means we'll enter a year of Jubilee in September of 2015!

In God's mind, rest is an act of worship not just cessation from labor. When we enter into God's rest, we pause in the midst of our busy lives and say to God, "I do not have what I have through my own labors. You are my Provider. I can rest and still prosper since you are my God."

In Jewish tradition, anyone who commits murder, idolatry, or sexual immorality is driven from the land—as is anyone who violates the laws of Shemitah! We know that more than once, God drove Israel from her land for violating the Sabbath.

It is wise to remember that God takes His Sabbaths—His weekly Sabbath, His seven-year Sabbath, and His fifty-year Sabbath—very seriously. They are "holy unto the Lord."

So what are we to make of all this?

First, let me be very clear, I am not among those who claim doom and gloom on the basis of Red Blood Moons. I believe that an apocalyptic industry is operating in our world that draws a huge amount of attention by making outlandish claims at the slightest provocation, generating fear, confusion, and retreat from God's people, rather than the victory that is ours as believers in Jesus Christ.

Second, I see two lines of evidence confirming that God does not want us to respond to the events going on around us with fear and trembling. The first line of evidence is the clear testimony of the Word of God, in passages such as these:

> God has not appointed us to wrath.
>
> —1 THESSALONIANS 5:9

> The path of the just is as the shining light, that shines more and more unto the perfect day.
>
> —PROVERBS 4:18

> For God has not given us the spirit of fear, but of power, and love, and self-control.
>
> —2 TIMOTHY 1:7

> Perfect love casts out fear.
>
> —1 JOHN 4:18

Additionally, we need to understand that God gives us a choice about how we are going to react to the signs of the times. Historically, one of the greatest controversies in the church world has been the tension between the sovereignty of God and man's free moral agency. Yet, God has given us both the right and the ability to choose what we are going to believe. Here's what Moses told the children of Israel, in Deuteronomy 30:19:

> I call heaven and earth to witnesses against you this day, that I have set before you life and death, blessing and curse. Therefore choose life, that both you and your descendants may live.

While there are those who attribute everything that happens in their lives to the usually ill-defined concept of destiny, I am convinced that whether or not God's will is done, either in an individual life or in a nation, has much more to do with decisions than destiny.

The second line of evidence confirming that God does not want us to respond to the events going on around us with fear comes from our knowledge that our heavenly Father is a loving Father. He wants us to be looking up instead of down, forward instead of backward, anticipating His blessings instead of curses. We are His new covenant people, with the shed blood of the Lamb covering our doorposts!

According to the Jewish calendar, this year, 2015 on the Gregorian calendar, is actually the year 5775 on God's calendar, and it begins at Rosh Hashanah 2015. Keep in mind that all letters in the Hebrew alphabet have a numeric value assigned to them, as well as a pictorial symbol.

The symbol for the Hebrew number 70, which is the decade in which we're living according to the Jewish calendar, is the letter *ayin* (aye-EEN). The pictorial form of *ayin* is a symbol with two heads, or eyes, on top that indicate seeing, understanding, and obeying the prophetic insight available to us. Two eyes indicate a choice that must be made: we can approach our future with either fear or faith—with a positive expectation or a negative attitude. The choice is ours. The direction of our lives and the outcomes we experience are, in most cases, a direct result of the way we choose to look at the circumstances around us.

Be encouraged, my friends. Our mighty God rules and reigns over all His creation, and He has your good in mind. If you look for His good, you will find it, whether in the everyday affairs of life or in the signs in the heavens.

I like to tell the story of the twin boys who wanted a pony for Christmas. On Christmas morning, their parents took them to a barn and opened a stall door to reveal a stall that was packed with horse manure. The pessimistic twin began to complain, saying, "This is terrible! I never get what I want!"

His brother, the optimistic twin, didn't complain. He just grabbed a shovel and began digging.

The pessimistic twin said, "What in the world are you doing? This is nothing but a big mess!" His optimistic brother replied, "With all this manure, there's got to be a pony in here somewhere!"

Your circumstances may be much better than a stall full of manure, or much worse. But, whatever the case, when you look for God's goodness, you *will* find it, even in the most desperate of times.

The Red Blood Moons of 2014 and 2015 are not last-minute announcements of judgment that caught God off guard. Quite the contrary, they are signs that God set in motion from the beginning of creation. More specifically, the truth is, that anything taking place in the heavens today was put in place and set in motion by God on the fourth day of creation.

God is not angry with us. He loves us and can't stop loving us! He tells us as much in Romans 5:5–9:

> And hope does not disappoint, because the love of God is
> shed abroad in our hearts by the Holy Spirit who has been

given to us. While we were yet weak, in due time Christ died for the ungodly. Rarely for a righteous man will one die. Yet perhaps for a good man some would even dare to die. But God demonstrates His own love toward us, in that while we were yet sinners, Christ died for us. How much more then, being now justified by His blood, shall we be saved from wrath through Him.

Remember, our heavenly Father's purpose is to bless us, because we are His beloved sons and daughters. He desires that we draw near to Him, not shrink away in fear.

I believe that God's celestial signs in the skies and the unusual alignment of heavenly bodies and earthly dates that we experience are evidence of God's love and desire to bless His people in the midst of a tortured and troubled world.

Certainly God's holiness compels Him to deal with the sin of the world, but God's wrath does not rest upon us. It rested on Jesus Christ. Our sins are forgiven in Him. He was nailed to the cross in our place. What rests upon us is God's love, and that is glorious news!

Let's remember that while this latest tetrad of Red Blood Moons aligned with God's feast dates, that September 2014 to September 2015 was a Shemitah year—a year of rest, provision, liberty, and peace for God's people; and September 2015 to September 2016 is a Jubilee year—a year of supernatural debt cancellation where the free favors of God are ours! Could it be that God placed the alignment of Red Blood Moons with His feasts in 2014 and 2015 to remind us of these very facts? Wouldn't it be just like our great God and loving heavenly Father to write of His love for us on the scroll of the heavens, just to reassure us as we live in this tumultuous generation?

Perhaps He wanted to remind us of the week of creation. Perhaps He wanted to remind us that He holds all things together by the power of His word (Hebrews 1:3). Perhaps He is saying, "I am here, and I have you in the palm of My hand. Fear not!" I believe this is what God is saying. In fact, I am sure of it!

Perhaps Jesus will seize the opportunity to make His second advent on the Feast of Trumpets. It would be scripturally accurate and make perfect sense for our Canaan King, Jesus Christ, to make His triumphant return to Earth during the feast season of Tabernacles, perhaps during the Feast of Trumpets, splitting the eastern skies and riding on that steaming white stallion, (See Revelation 19:11.) Wouldn't that be something?

Let me tell you, though, I'm not about to make any such prediction! Christians have embarrassed themselves too many times through the years by trying to predict when Jesus will return. I don't plan to join their number. I do, however, plan to be purified by the hope of His appearing, and you will find me saying quite often—nearly every day of my life—"Even so, come quickly, Lord Jesus." But don't leave these pages thinking I've predicted the return of Christ. I haven't. I'm just eager for my Lord to return.

Here is my prediction, and I urge you to make it your prediction *and* confession: "Jesus is coming back—and until He does, I plan to walk in His blessing and serve Him with every fiber of my being. Even so, come, Lord Jesus!"

PART TWO

SET
APPOINTMENTS
WITH GOD

Chapter 4

FREEDOM IS YOURS

*Hear, O Israel: The L*ORD *is our God. The L*ORD *is one!
And you shall love the L*ORD *your God with all your
heart and with all your soul and with all your might.*

DEUTERONOMY 6:4–5

THESE ARE THE WORDS OF THE GREAT *SHEMA* (SHEH-MAH) of Deuteronomy 6:4, perhaps the most cherished verse of the Torah through the centuries. With these words, the Feast of the Passover is inaugurated.

After these words are spoken, at exactly eighteen minutes before sundown on Nisan 15 in Jewish homes the world over, the eldest woman of the house lights the Passover candles. According to tradition, she welcomes the holiday, first by waving her hands over the flames three times and covering her eyes so as not to see the candles burning, and then by reciting these ancient words: "Blessed art thou, Lord our God, Master of the universe, who sanctifies us with Thy commandments, and commanded us to kindle the light (of Shabbat and of) the holiday."[1]

Next, she reaches for "Miriam's Cup" and passes it to the other women at the table to fill with water from their own glasses. When the cup is full, a blessing is read: "This is the cup of Miriam, a cup of living water. A reminder of the Exodus from Egypt."[2]

And thus the Passover Seder (SAY-duhr), the Feast of Our Freedom, begins.

My heart stirs each time I hear the beautiful words of the Shema. The name for this verse comes from its first two words in the original Hebrew: *"Shema Yisrael"* or "Hear, O Israel."

From the day of Adam to the final trumpet, this is the call of God upon the human heart. When one of the Pharisees asked Jesus, "Teacher, which is the greatest commandment in the law?" (Matthew 22:36), He answered by quoting the *Shema.* His words encapsulate all that God asks of those who serve Him.

The Shema is prayed each morning and each evening during the Passover celebration, and on all the sacred days that follow it. It inaugurates the Feast of Passover each year, as it has done for generations. It stirs the hearts of men to know their God, to love Him unreservedly, and to offer before Him all of their gifts and their deepest hopes.

I see it as very right and fitting that these stirring words of the Shema should be wrapped around the Great Feast, for Passover is the feast of God's redemption—a redemption that deserves to be answered just as the *Shema* describes: by hearing God's Word more carefully, by loving the Lord more fully, and by sacrificing before Him more completely.

Passover is one of the three Pilgrim festivals of the Jewish faith, celebrating the exodus of the Jewish people from slavery in Egypt. From the very beginning of Israel's history, God was at work, instituting the festivals and ceremonies that would burn His truth into the hearts of generations of His people. He didn't wait until Egypt was struck down and the Israelites were safely in the Promised Land. He gave His instructions for the first Passover in Egypt immediately after it occurred. These instructions remain the same for us today, centuries later, because He intends for us to celebrate His Passover for all time.

You likely already know the story of Israel's first Passover, but I invite you to come with me now, and explore once again the historic moment in which a people born of the family of a single man were transformed into a nation that forever changed the world.

According to scholars, the great Exodus of Israel out of Egypt likely occurred in 1446 BC. Though the wise Hebrew ruler Joseph had once saved all of Egypt, bringing honor to the Jewish people, the good he had accomplished was eventually forgotten. The Bible tells us that there arose in Egypt a Pharaoh who "knew not Joseph" (Exodus 1:8) and did not remember or honor the salvation won at Joseph's hand. This new Pharaoh and all those who came after him for the next 430 years gave the Jews only the shackle and the lash. Egypt enslaved the Hebrews, making them objects of hatred and abuse.

The Hebrews became a people without heritage, without legacy, without possessions, without reward for their labors, and seemingly without any greater purpose in the world than to build the idolatrous monuments of Egypt. They suffered greatly at the hands of the Egyptians, until Moses came and spoke God's fierce command to Pharaoh, saying, "Let my people go!" But Pharaoh's heart was hardened, devoted to his false gods, and he would not listen.

In response, God sent ten plagues upon the land. Water turned to blood, and the land and all upon it were beset by frogs, lice, flies, boils, hail, locusts, and darkness. All except the Hebrews, whom God spared. In the midst of these plagues, they lived in divine protection, in the land of Goshen provided for them by God. And still, Pharaoh's heart grew harder.

And so, God visited the tenth and most deadly plague upon Egypt: the killing of the firstborn of the land. In Exodus 12:2–8,

God gives His instructions to Moses so that the Hebrews may be protected from this last and most awful of plagues:

> This month shall be the beginning of months to you. It shall be the first month of the year to you. Speak to all the congregation of Israel, saying: On the tenth day of this month every man shall take a lamb, according to the house of their fathers, a lamb for a household....
>
> You shall keep it up until the fourteenth day of the same month, and then the whole assembly of the congregation of Israel shall kill it in the evening. They shall take some of the blood and put it on the two side posts and on the upper doorpost of the houses in which they shall eat it.

The Israelites did as God commanded, and God kept His promise. The firstborn of Egypt died that night but not the firstborn of the Hebrews. Not a single Egyptian family was left untouched by death, "and there was loud wailing in Egypt" (Exodus 12:30).

The next morning, Pharaoh begged the people of God to leave Egypt, the land of their bondage. The Israelites were more than happy to comply, and so they left, taking with them the wealth the Egyptians heaped upon them. But then, Pharaoh decided to pursue them with his army. Thankfully the Israelites escaped through the Red Sea as God miraculously parted the waters for them, while swallowing up Pharaoh and his armies in the swirling waves once the people of God were safe on dry land.

Thus began the wilderness wanderings of the people of God that would eventually fashion them into a people prepared to occupy a land of their own. It took time—far too much time due to their rebellion and idolatry—but the day came when they finally entered the Promised Land, and a nation was born out of bondage.

A PATTERN FOR ALL GENERATIONS

Clearly God was fashioning more than a one-time deliverance in 1446 BC. As He instructed Moses about what should be done at that critical moment in Egypt, He was creating the pattern for Passovers for all time. That is why, before He spoke of lambs and blood on doorposts, He first said, "This month shall be the beginning of months to you. It shall be the first month of the year to you. Speak to all the congregation of Israel, saying: On the tenth day of this month..." (Exodus 12:2–3).

The Hebrew calendar begins with the month of Nisan, just as the event that first happened in the month of Nisan started the Hebrew people as a nation. It was on the tenth of this month that the Hebrew people would choose their lambs. On the fourteenth of this month that these lambs would be sacrificed and the blood placed upon the doorposts of every Hebrew home. This month and these dates would be remembered forever and relived in Passover observances for generations to come.

I love that there is meaning in each detail. Notice, for example, that each Hebrew family would choose its lamb and live with it for four days before sacrificing it to God. Because the Hebrews were shepherds, they were close to their flocks and knew their sacrificial lamb intimately. In fact they were commanded to know it, commanded to be sure that the sacrifice had no blemishes.

It's interesting to note the fact that, during the time of their enslavement in Egypt, many of the Israelites were shepherds, which made them even more of a stench in the nostrils of the Egyptians. Our Bible tells us that the very reason that the Hebrews lived in the region of Egypt called Goshen, removed from the Egyptian people, was that "all shepherds are detestable to the Egyptians" (Genesis 46:34, NIV).

But on that first Passover in Egypt, everything was changing and changing quickly. Calamity was about to befall Egypt. The people of Israel were shortly to pull up stakes and leave the land where they endured centuries of slavery, and yet God, who is never in a hurry, calmly gave Moses instructions for the Passover observances that defined generations yet to come:

> You shall observe this thing as an ordinance to you and to your sons forever. When you enter the land which the Lord will give you, according as He has promised, that you shall observe this service. And when your children shall say to you, "What does this service mean to you?" that you shall say, "It is the sacrifice of the Lord's Passover, who passed over the houses of the children of Israel in Egypt, when He smote the Egyptians, and delivered our households."
>
> —EXODUS 12:24–27

Our God, who thinks in times and seasons and cycles, was from the very beginning of Israel's story instituting the festivals and ceremonies that would burn His truth into the hearts of generations of His people.

THE LAMB OF GOD

Before we go further, I want to make sure you know the most important truth of Passover—the true "Lamb of God" is Jesus Christ, the Son of the living God. How thrilling this is for believers living in the new covenant!

John the Baptist identified Jesus with these words: "Look, the Lamb of God, who takes away the sin of the world" (John 1:29). The Book of Revelation gives us this description of Jesus seated at the right hand of God:

> I saw a Lamb in the midst of the throne and of the four living creatures, and in the midst of the elders, standing as though

it had been slain, having seven horns and seven eyes, which are the seven Spirits of God, sent out into all the earth. He came and took the scroll out of the right hand of Him who sat on the throne.

When He had taken the scroll, the four living creatures and the twenty-four elders fell down before the Lamb, each one having a harp, and golden bowls full of incense, which are the prayers of saints. And they sang a new song, saying: "You are worthy to take the scroll, and to open its seals; for You were slain, and have redeemed us to God by Your blood out of every tribe and tongue and people and nation, and have made us kings and priests unto our God; and we shall reign on the earth."

Then I looked, and I heard around the throne and the living creatures and the elders the voices of many angels, numbering ten thousand times ten thousand, and thousands of thousands, saying with a loud voice: "Worthy is the Lamb who was slain, to receive power and riches and wisdom and strength and honor and glory and blessing!"

Then I heard every creature which is in heaven and on the earth and under the earth and in the sea, and all that are in them, saying: "To Him who sits on the throne and to the Lamb be blessing and honor and glory and power, forever and ever!"

—Revelation 5:6–13

Every Passover celebrated through the centuries points to Jesus. Indeed, the heart of our message as Christians is that the Lamb of God has been slain for the sins of the world, and this same Lamb now reigns in heaven. Never let us forget: Jesus is the Lamb of God! Paul declared it for all time: "For even Christ, our Passover, has been sacrificed" (1 Corinthians 5:7).

My purpose in telling you about Passover is that, just as the blood of the lamb was placed upon the doorposts and lintels of the Hebrew houses in Egypt, you also might be cleansed by the blood of the Lamb of God. Passover is so much more than an historical feast. It is recognition and honor of the saving blood of Jesus Christ.

As Christians, when we take the bread and wine of Passover as communion, we do so in remembrance of Jesus, whose body and blood have delivered us from sin and death, just as the blood of the lamb delivered the Israelites in Egypt.

You see, it is so important for us to be radical and unashamed about this matter of the blood of the Lamb. God used bold terms when He commanded that the blood was to be placed on the homes of the Hebrews. First, He instructed that the blood be applied with hyssop, which is a long, bushy plant that is highly aromatic.

Once it had been dipped in the blood of the sacrificed lambs, this hyssop would apply the blood in huge swaths. The doorposts were not to be covered with little paintbrush-sized streaks of blood. No, the original Hebrew uses the word *paint* to describe the way the blood should be applied. Picture big, bold, unmistakable splashes of blood.

Why so much emphasis on the blood? Because, the blood of the Lamb (Jesus Christ) washes our sin away and leaves us protected from the curse. We should never be hesitant about the blood, or slow to claim its power for ourselves. Without the shedding of blood, there is no remission of sin (Hebrews 9:22). This is why our dear Savior was so horribly wounded—to shed the blood that would set us free.

I invite you to take a moment sometime in the near future to examine the whole text of Isaiah 53. As much as you may want to shy away, I urge you to read and contemplate the description of Jesus being savaged and brutalized. He endured this for you, so the blood He spilled could be applied to your life.

David knew what the blood could do, even in his day, before the Son of God shed the most precious blood of all. In repentance after his vile adultery, he cried out to God and said, "Purify me with hyssop, and I will be clean; wash me, and I will be whiter than snow" (Psalm 51:7).

I want to share a few quotes from my book, *The Cross: One Man, One Tree, One Friday,* to help remind you of the excruciating suffering our Lord endured during His crucifixion. Many will find this almost too difficult to contemplate, but Jesus did not just contemplate it, He endured every minute of it, for you and for me.

> As we stand watching, in stupefied horror, inconspicuously amid the crowd of gawkers, the Son of God—the one who spoke with such power and poetry about the way God clothes the lilies of the field with beauty—is stripped naked. He is forced to face a massive stone column and leather straps are attached to His wrists, allowing soldiers to stretch His beloved arms that were strong enough to stop the tempestuous sea and gentle enough to hold the little children around the curve of the column and thereby stretching the skin of His back taut.
>
> The cursed whip consists of several strips of leather with a series of stone beads or metal balls spaced periodically along the length of each strand. At the tip of each strip is a jagged fragment of sheep bone hewn and filed sharp as a razor. The wielder of the whip is an expert in his ghastly craft—trained to inflict maximum pain and damage but without killing his victim.[3]
>
> Finally, and suddenly, it is over. The volume of blood now pooled around the base of the column is astonishing. His piercing eyes are now swollen shut from repeated blows from dozens of fists, beard partially yanked out at the roots, and

the devastating effects of the flogging have rendered Jesus of Nazareth essentially unrecognizable. Even so, the worst is yet to come.

The woven ring of thorns is jammed brutally down upon His hemorrhaging brow and the robe is thrown over the raw and torn flesh of His blood-soaked back. We witness another demon-inspired round of spitting, punching and taunting before the robe is ripped from his back, reopening His wounds, and is replaced by a roughhewn wooden cross beam which, in His deplorable and depleted condition, He must now carry.[4]

We witness in anguish as Jesus is hurled to the ground and roughly stretched out upon the cross beam which had been delivered and deposited by Simon. A five-inch-long spike is struck by an anvil driving it crashing through sinews and flesh. As His nerves contort, in horrible spasms, with great precision, both nails find their marks in each wrist just below the base of the hand and sink deeply into the wooden beam.

Then, with aid of ropes and pulleys, the beam, with man attached, is hoisted up and into place atop the vertical post. The force of the beam dropping into place immediately jerks both arms out of their shoulder sockets. Jesus, our Savior, dangles there momentarily, but the Flesh Nailer has two more spikes in his hand.

He takes hold of one of Jesus' feet and positions it, not at the front of the vertical beam but at the side. Then he drives the spike sideways, through the thickest portion of the ankle bone, and on into the post. He repeats this with the other foot on the other side of the post.[5]

Even now, as you read these words, ask God to be your Passover once again. Ask Him to apply the powerful blood of Jesus in generous amounts to the mounting sin in your life, and the cleansing will come and the curse will pass you by. The Lamb of God will enter your life and make you who you are meant to be, a much loved son or daughter in service to the living God.

I want us to move now into an examination of the joyous celebration of the Feast of Passover itself as it was and is practiced today. There is so much for us to learn here, so much for us to appreciate. This "Feast of Our Freedom" is a liturgy of sorts, which evolved down through the centuries through the efforts of the rabbis, to symbolize the Passover story for all generations.

THE FEAST OF PASSOVER

Beginning the second year after the Exodus of Israel from Egypt, the Hebrew people began celebrating the Feast of Passover. They would call it *Pesach* (PAY-sahk), the Hebrew word for "pass over."

Can you imagine their joy as they wandered in the wilderness of Sinai, enjoying the privilege of reenacting and celebrating their deliverance from Egypt? They had been delivered from bondage and made into a people set apart for God. What delight!

Passover would begin, as it had in Egypt, at twilight on the fourteenth of the first month, or Nisan, with each Hebrew family choosing its unblemished lamb four days prior. Then, on the sacred day, the lamb was sacrificed and cooked for the evening meal. The Passover would then begin and proceed as God had commanded Moses at the first Passover:

> They shall eat the flesh on that night, roasted with fire, and
> they shall eat it with unleavened bread and bitter herbs. Do
> not eat it raw, nor boiled at all with water, but roasted with
> fire, its head with its legs and its entrails. And you shall let
> nothing of it remain until the morning, but that of it which
> remains until the morning you shall burn with fire. In this
> way shall you eat it: with your waist girded, your sandals on

your feet, and your staff in your hand. So you shall eat it in haste. It is the LORD's Passover.

—EXODUS 12:8–11

It was a joyous occasion but always conducted with the utmost seriousness, because observing Passover was a command of God that kept people cleansed from sin. "The man who…fails to keep the Passover, even the same person will be cut off from his people. Because he did not bring the offering of the LORD at its appointed time, that man will bear his sin" (Numbers 9:13). Remember, under the old covenant, you had to be continually washed clean of sin because there had not yet been the once and for all sacrifice of Jesus, the precious Lamb of God who took away the sins of the world.

THE "LITURGY" OF THE PASSOVER SEDER

What we Christians call the Last Supper was, for Jesus and His disciples, a Passover meal. Our Jewish friends call this meal a *Seder*, which means "order" or "arrangement." This sacred meal has evolved through the centuries for the observance of the Passover feast.

The Passover meal is to be celebrated by the entire family, with everyone taking part. It begins with a blessing that prepares the family for the sacredness of this holiday. The eldest woman of the household, usually the wife, begins the service with the lighting of the traditional Passover candles, followed by the prayer of blessings: "Blessed art Thou, O Lord, King of the Universe, who sanctifies us by Thy commandment and commands us to light the Lights of the Passover." The Messianic version of this blessing acknowledges Jesus our Messiah as the Light of the world: "Blessed are You, Lord our God, King of the universe, who sancti-fied us with his commandments, and commanded us to be a light to the nations and who gave to us Jesus our Messiah the Light of the world."

One of the distinctive features of the Passover meal is its educational aspect. God instructed Moses to make sure the young were taught about this holy night of Passover:

> And when your children shall say to you, "What does this service mean to you?" that you shall say, "It is the sacrifice of the LORD's Passover, who passed over the houses of the children of Israel in Egypt, when He smote the Egyptians."
> —EXODUS 12:26

The Passover includes dramas that members of the family play out. There is a role for a wise child, a wicked child, a simple child, and a foolish child. Each one has a speaking part in what amounts to a type of family skit. There are also object lessons drawn from the various foods that are eaten, and from the water and wine. Unleavened bread called *matzo* (MAHT-zoh) is used, along with eggs, cloth, salt, and the shank of the lamb. All of this is designed to teach the next generation the core truth of God's care for His people.

The heart of this truth is surveyed in Deuteronomy 6:20–25:

> When your son asks you in time to come, saying, "What do the testimonies and the statutes and the judgments mean which the LORD our God has commanded you?" then you shall say to your son, "We were slaves of Pharaoh in Egypt, and the LORD brought us out of Egypt with a mighty hand. And the LORD showed great and devastating signs and wonders upon Egypt, upon Pharaoh, and upon all his household before our eyes. He brought us out from there, so that He might bring us in, to give us the land which He swore to our fathers. The LORD commanded us to do all these statutes, to fear the LORD our God, for our good always, that He

might preserve us, as He has to this day. It will be our righteousness if we are careful to keep all these commandments before the LORD our God, just as He has commanded us."

THE CUPS OF WINE

One of the most important traditions that evolved around the Passover meal has to do with wine. There are four cups of wine used in the Seder to symbolize the four promises made by God as found in the sixth chapter of Exodus. This is important to us because it is a tradition that Jesus used to explain the meaning of His sacrifice to His disciples, and to the world.

The Jews evolved a practice of using four cups of wine as symbols of God's provision, to celebrate the promises of Exodus 6:6–7. Notice that there are five "I will" statements in these verses.

> Therefore say to the children of Israel: "I am the LORD, and I will bring you out from under the burdens of the Egyptians, and I will rid you out of their bondage, and I will redeem you with a stretched-out arm and with great judgments. And I will take you to Me for a people, and I will be to you a God. And you shall know that I am the LORD your God, who brings you out from under the burdens of the Egyptians."

The Cup of Consecration

The first cup of wine is known as the Cup of Consecration and is used to celebrate the truth of "I will bring you out." It is consumed in celebration of the tremendous mercy of God, who delivered His people from bondage in Egypt. This is a mercy that calls for sanctification. The words: "God brought us out, let us consecrate ourselves to Him," live in the minds of the Jewish people.

The Cup of Deliverance

The second cup of wine is known as the Cup of Deliverance. It is based on the promise "I will deliver you from Egyptian slavery, I will free you from bondage." The celebration of this cup is two-fold: it celebrates that God has removed His people from Egypt, *and* that the spirit of Egypt and the ways of Egypt were also removed from the hearts of God's people.

The Cup of Deliverance complements the Cup of Consecration. It is a declaration that deliverance is complete, that Israel is delivered from Egypt and Egypt is also taken out of Israel.

The Cup of Redemption

The third cup of wine is the Cup of Redemption. This cup is used to celebrate the promise "I will redeem you with My power." This meant that God would pay any price to stretch out His arm, destroy all enemies, and make Israel His people. He would stop at nothing to make Israel His own. The emphasis here is upon an act of redemption, the act of paying a price to deliver or rescue.

Before we examine the fourth cup of wine, I want to turn our attention to a passage in the Gospel of Luke, where Jesus, at the Last Supper (the Passover) used the third cup to reveal what was about to happen.

In Luke 22:20, we are told that as Jesus sat at the table of the Passover meal, He took the third cup into His hand and said, "This cup is the new covenant in My blood which is shed for you."

Let's stop and think about this for a moment. Here are a group of Jews whose culture has celebrated Passover for centuries by eating lamb with bitter herbs as they remember their national birth in the deliverance from Egypt. And for centuries, they have consumed four cups of wine in honor of God's great provision as described in Exodus 6.

And now, here is Jesus, on this sacred night, the night of the last

Passover He would ever celebrate during His life on Earth, taking the third cup of wine—the Cup of Redemption—and declaring Himself the fulfillment of its meaning! Can you imagine what His disciples must have been thinking?

No doubt they could not even begin to comprehend what Jesus was telling them, that their heavenly Father would spare no expense to fashion a people of His own. At that very moment, God was preparing to pay the final price with the blood of His Son.

This third cup, the Cup of Redemption that Jesus offered up to His disciples in that upper room, was actually the cup of the new covenant, about to be purchased with His precious blood and given graciously by a loving heavenly Father for each one of us.

I cannot write these words without weeping at this glorious truth that echoes down through the ages. Jesus is the Passover! He is the Lamb of God! His blood is the once and for all sacrifice that makes all other sacrifices obsolete! His blood redeems. His blood cleanses. His blood makes right what has been destroyed through sin. And He invites each one of us to drink the cup of His blood and be liberated by the living God, just as the children of Israel were liberated in Egypt of old.

Mishnah (MEESH-nah)

I want to pause for a moment here and examine an important aspect of the Cup of Redemption. In the record of the teachings of the ancient rabbis, which is called the *Mishnah*, we are told "the Passover wine was said to be red and was to be mixed with warm water."[6]

Ask a rabbi why wine and warm water are mixed, and he will tell you that this mixture of blood and water produces a closer representation of the blood of the Passover Lamb. This ancient tradition begs us to remember that tragic day when the perfect and precious Lamb of God was sacrificed.

Jesus had hung on that rugged cross for six excruciating hours.

He had just uttered the sacred words, "It is finished," and Mary, His mother, who watched Him take His first breath, wept as He exhaled His last, thus completing His Father's master plan to redeem this cursed planet and the souls of men.

We are told in John 19:33–34 that when the Roman soldiers approached the body of Jesus on the cross, they saw that He was dead already, and so they did not break His legs. But one of the soldiers pierced His side with a spear and out poured blood and water.

Think of it: through all of the centuries, God's covenant people drank a ceremonial cup of wine mixed with water and called it a "Cup of Redemption," foreshadowing what they could never have conceived—that Jesus, the sinless Lamb of God, the final Passover sacrifice, would pour out His blood mixed with water on the cross of Calvary.

Jesus's last words on the cross, "It is finished," carry a greater meaning that many of us know. Once again, allow me to quote from *The Cross: One Man, One Tree, One Friday*, regarding this powerful and prophetic statement, so that you may understand the fullness of its meaning.

> When John, the beloved disciple, recalls this statement to record it in his gospel narrative, he uses a Greek accounting term—*tetelestai*. Future English translations of John's Gospel will render that term in a way that tends to strip it of the legal and financial connotations.
>
> They translate it, "It is finished" (three words for one). But *tetelestai* does not mean merely that a thing has ended. It has a far greater implication than merely a clock has run out and the game has concluded. It is a declaration that all has been accomplished.
>
> All that was lacking has now been supplied. The breach

has been healed. The debt has been fully satisfied. Shalom—nothing broken, nothing missing.[7]

Truly, Jesus's death on the cross is a finished and complete work. Our debt has been fully satisfied. Jesus understood this and told us so in His last words on Earth before His death.

The Fourth Cup

And what of that fourth cup of wine, the Cup of Praise? In Hebrew the word for "praise" is *hallel* (hah-LEHL), and so this cup is often referred to even in English as the "Cup of Hallel." It is the cup consumed in honor of God's promise, "I will take you to Me as My people."

From the biblical narrative we see that Jesus did not drink this fourth cup on that final Passover of His earthly life. After drinking the third cup at that Last Supper, Jesus and His disciples rose, sang a hymn, and made their way to the Garden of Gethsemane. The fourth cup of wine, this Cup of Praise, sat on the table in the upper room while Jesus went out into the night. What should this mean to us?

Remember the theme of the fourth cup: "I will take you to Me as My people." This fourth cup is the cup of the marriage feast, to be consumed when Jesus takes His bride, the church, and the wedding celebration of the Lamb commences. Jesus was referring to this cup when He said,

> For this is My blood of the new covenant, which is shed for many for the remission of sins. I say to you, I will not drink of this fruit of the vine from now on until that day when I drink it new with you in My Father's kingdom.
> —MATTHEW 26:28–29

Just think of it: a party awaits us! It is the grand ball that will begin when Jesus comes for His church, His bride without spot or wrinkle, and takes her for His own. He has already paid the price. What remains is for the wedding of the Lamb and His bride. On that day, we will all drink that fourth Cup of Praise (hallel) in the kingdom of God and we will dance. Oh, how we will dance!

THE PROMISES OF PASSOVER
FROM EXODUS 23

In Exodus 23:20–30, we find seven wonderful promises from God's Word concerning His Passover feast, or Pesach, that will enhance your spiritual life if you will participate in and claim these truths as your own at this appointed time on God's calendar.

1. God promises He will dispatch an angel on your behalf in Exodus 23:20, "Indeed, I am going to send an angel before you to guard you along the way and to bring you into the place which I have prepared." God will commission legions of angels that are only assigned to you during the days leading up to and including the season of Passover. Psalm 103:20 reminds us that His angels "obey the voice of His word" so take this opportunity to commission these divine servants using the Word of God!

   We also see many times in Scripture that God released angels at this specific time of year for those in need who were observing this feast season. In Luke 22:42, God dispatched an angel to Jesus Himself to minister strength to Him just after He prayed in the garden, "Father, if You are willing, remove this cup from Me. Nevertheless not My will, but Yours, be done." When Peter was in jail, the night before he was scheduled to go to trial, we know from Acts 12 that God sent an angel and helped him escape in the midst of sixteen Roman guards. And in 2 Kings 19, an angel was dispatched on behalf of Hezekiah and smote one hundred eighty five thousand of his enemies!

2. The Lord promises to be an adversary to your adversaries and an enemy to your enemies. Exodus 23:22 says: "If you diligently obey his voice and do all that I say, then I will be an enemy to your enemies and an adversary to your adversaries." The God that has been fighting *with* you is about to fight *for* you! Passover is a strategic season of opportunity when God will step into the arena of your conflict, and your enemy will come up against a God with whom He cannot contend.

   Isaiah 54:14 promises that we shall be far from oppression, we shall not fear, and terror will not come near us. That literally means our enemy will stay far from us, we will live in peace, and the spirit of fear will not come nigh us. Isaiah 41:10 plainly tells us, "Do not fear!" I pray these Scriptures daily and command the spirit of fear to be supernaturally extracted from the children of God as they continually build and use their faith, which cannot fail because the Son of God is at the Father's right hand making intercession for us even now!

3. God will provide assets, meaning that which is necessary, for you. Exodus 23:25 says, "He shall bless your bread and your water." Our God is a God of provision, and you can rest assured knowing He will provide your basic needs like food, water, shelter, and finances to pay your bills.

Not only that, but Ezekiel 47:12 tells us that the trees by the river shall bring forth new fruit every month. How often do your bills come due? Every month. Talk about perpetual blessing! Psalm 1:3 reiterates this truth by reminding us that whatsoever we do, shall prosper.

4. God will remove affliction from your midst. In other words, divine healing will be manifested! It is found in Exodus 23:25, "And I will remove sickness from your midst."

    First Peter 2:24 echoes the words of the prophet Isaiah when he says, "By His wounds you were healed." Healing is not a promise; healing is a fact. It is an established reality. You have been healed!

5. Another wonderful promise is that you will become ageless. Exodus 23:26, "No one shall be miscarrying or be barren in your land. I will fulfill the number of your days." Man's been searching for the secret to longevity and youthfulness since the beginning of time—from Ponce de Leon's attempt to discover the fountain of youth to today's advanced medical procedures to turn back the hands of time. Of course, no one is getting off this planet alive, unless Jesus returns for us in the rapture, but God wants to reassure us that we can live long, happy, and healthy lives. We don't have to die under the grip of sickness or in an accident!

    Psalm 91:16 says, "With long life will I satisfy him…" What a glorious promise from God's Word, but we must also do our part to keep our bodies and minds healthy by eating correctly, exercising, and using wisdom in all things.

6. God promises to give you abundance in this season—beyond what is necessary! Exodus 23:30 reminds us "…until you become fruitful and inherit the land." And Genesis 8:22 records this eternal law of God's kingdom; "While the earth remains, seedtime and harvest." That's not an accurate translation. The Bible does not say seedtime and harvest. The *and* was added. It is not seedtime and harvest, because that makes you think that you sow the seed, and then somewhere down the road there's a harvest.

We serve an infinite God. He is not alpha and omega. He is Alpha-Omega and Omega-Alpha. You can't tell the beginning from the end. There will come a time that what you call the end, God will call the beginning! So we can proclaim by the promise of the Passover anointing that "He is a God of abundance, and He is my God!"

7. God will give us an alpha year. Exodus 23:29 says, "I will not drive them out before you in one year…" and Exodus 23:30 states, "Little by little I will drive them out before you…" This is a year that will affect all future years. This year you will receive a revelation that changes everything forever!

In Exodus 12:2 God said, "This month shall be the beginning of months to you. It shall be the first month of the year to you." In other words, what we call the end, God calls the beginning! And Psalm 105:37 recounts that during the Passover, "He brought them out with silver and gold, and no one among their tribes faltered."

These promises are for us, God's children, who adhere to and recognize His sacred feast of Pesach. I pray you receive each one of these revelations as your very own, claim their promises according to the Word, and receive the manifestations of them in your life.

Chapter 5

SECOND CHANCES ARE GOD'S SPECIALTY

Pesach is not only about "freedom from." It is about
our having the freedom to make the world a more
sacred place by expanding God's presence in it.[1]
Rabbi David A. Teutsch

Moses and the Israelites were in the desert of Sinai. It was the first month of the second year since they had been delivered out of Egypt. God told Moses to have the people celebrate Passover at twilight on the fourteenth day of the month, according to His instructions.

All was well with the Passover celebration until some men came to Moses and Aaron with a complaint. In the natural course of life, some of their tribe had passed away, and in the process of dealing with the bodies, the men had become ceremonially unclean, unfit to celebrate the Passover. This meant they could be cut off from their people and have to bear their own sins because they hadn't brought their Passover offering in its appointed season, according to Numbers 9:13. So they asked, "Should we be kept from the Lord's Passover?"

Now Moses, a humble man, didn't know the answer to this

dilemma, so he instructed the people to wait while he sought the Lord. When Moses returned, this is what he told the people:

> If any man of you or of your posterity is unclean because of a dead body, or is far off on a journey, he will still keep the Passover to the LORD. The fourteenth day of the second month at evening they will keep it, and eat it with unleavened bread and bitter herbs. They will leave none of it until the morning, nor break any of its bones. According to all the ordinances of the Passover they will keep it. But the man who is ceremonially clean, and is not on a journey, and fails to keep the Passover, even the same person will be cut off from his people. Because he did not bring the offering of the LORD at its appointed time, that man will bear his sin.
>
> —NUMBERS 9:10–13

This commandment from God created, in essence, a second Passover. The Hebrew for this second Passover is *Pesach Sheni* (PAY-sahk SHAY-nee), which literally means "second Passover." It occurs one month after the official Passover, on the fourteenth of the second month, in Iyar. This second Passover is for those who are away from the land on a journey, or who are ritually unclean when the Passover of the first month occurs.

We rarely hear Pesach Sheni mentioned, yet it has enormous potential to help us walk more fully in the majesty of Passover celebration, preparing us for a greater understanding of the Feast of Unleavened Bread that follows the day of Passover.

This second Passover is similar to the first Passover in many ways. Those who celebrate Pesach Sheni are to eat roasted lamb with bitter herbs in haste and with their cloaks tucked in, their sandals on their feet, and their staffs in their hands, as God had commanded. Yet there is one major difference in the two Passovers, and it involves leaven.

A primary feature of Passover is God's command that there should be no yeast eaten as part of the Passover meal. "They shall eat the flesh on that night, roasted with fire, and they shall eat it with unleavened bread and bitter herbs" (Exodus 12:8).

God wants yeast eliminated from the Passover meal because leaven is a symbol of sin in Scripture. Leaven, or yeast, is what causes bread to rise. It literally puffs up the bread. It is a living, growing organism that ferments and corrupts the bread flour. Isn't that the perfect picture of what sin does in our life?

By instructing His people to eliminate leaven from the Passover meal, God is using something in the natural to teach His spiritual principles. He is reminding His people to separate themselves from sin.

What is interesting about Pesach Sheni, the second Passover, is that it does not have the same restrictions regarding leaven. In fact, there are no restrictions about leaven being present when it comes to Pesach Sheni. There are no restrictions against owning leaven or even having leaven at your Passover table. One can eat the matzo or the unleavened bread, and with the very next bite, take a piece of leavened bread and consume that with the Passover lamb. There's no prohibition on leaven whatsoever when it comes to Pesach Sheni.

But why is this? Why is the symbolism of the wickedness of sin missing from the Second Passover?

I believe God is again speaking a mystery to us through the ancients. Leaven represents the human ego, self-will, and self-assertion. In the first Passover, God is saying, "Get rid of the leaven, get rid of your ego, and get rid of self and self-will." But in Pesach Sheni He is reminding us that our salvation is from Him, not from us. It is not something we "do." It is something He did.

With this one slight change in symbolism, God is teaching us what Martin Luther bled to learn, and generations have been bound up spiritually for forgetting, salvation is from the Lord. We didn't save ourselves. We can't get to heaven by conquering our sins in our own strength. It isn't as easy as getting some containers of yeast out of our homes.

No, you can't save yourself. You can't find the Lord. We don't know where to look for Him. Instead, out of the swirling ages of eternity past, He comes looking for us, treading the earthly way. Jesus is heaven come down, God incarnate, knocking on your heart. No man comes to God unless the Spirit draws him.

In short, Pesach Sheni, the second Passover, is about grace and second chances. It is about the fact that Jesus found me. He claimed me. He saved me. He washed me. He made me His own. I never could have saved myself. I never could have put the leaven out of my life as an act of my will. I am saved because God granted me His grace, the same kind of grace we see in Pesach Sheni, when the ban against leaven is lifted.

Put another way, the Passover celebration says to the Jew: "You had no more to do with being a Jew than you had to do with being born. So, how can you come with arrogance, with ego? You are a Jew because God reached down and delivered you by His mighty hand and made you His own, a people for Himself."

For a Christian, the message, particularly of this Pesach Sheni, is much the same. We didn't decide when we would come into relationship with Jesus. We were in darkness. We were strangers, aliens to the Commonwealth of Israel, and to the covenants of promise. They made no sense to us. Yet, right there in the middle of our mess, in the midst of our depravity, He came all the way down. He identified with us, laid His hand on our mouths and sanctified our lips, put His hand on our chests, and took out our stony hearts and put in a heart of flesh, so we could serve Him.

We are His because He chose us. He came to the dog pound of humanity and saw us and said, "That's the one I want." We were adopted. We got picked. We didn't have the right bloodline, but we got adopted anyway. How grateful we ought to be. It is by grace we are saved. We did not choose Jesus; He chose us.

God was doing miracles on Earth and in history, from the first feast in the first month at the beginning of the Hebrew calendar, but He wanted them commemorated in a way that prefigured Jesus, celebrated with lamb's blood, unleavened bread, bitter herbs, and wine. And then He instituted a second Passover, for the unclean, where the standards weren't as high, but the grace was just as deep. And He wanted all of this celebrated every year, so that the liberation of God might be declared before the nations of the world!

The two Passovers illustrate both the righteous standard of God: no leaven shall be among you in the first Passover, and the mystery of grace that even if there is leaven, God will save you anyway! He lovingly and graciously invites us to come under the blood, free of sin, into His mercy, where judgment and destruction will pass us by.

POSTSCRIPT JEHOVAH:
THE GOD OF THE SECOND CHANCE

A letter is a piece of correspondence wherein you communicate ideas or directives and then affix your signature to it, making it a legal document. It has the force of law if it has been administrated and signed. But then there's something called a postscript—a P.S.—in its abbreviated form. It is meant to add or even alter what's been communicated in the main body of the text.

We can liken this to Jesus, who came to fulfill the Law and sign a new treaty in His own blood. The Law needed to be altered so we could be offered a second chance, a mulligan, a do-over, if you will. The Bible is full of people just like you and me who received a second chance at the hand of a merciful God.

Moses, God's mighty right arm of deliverance, came into this earth at a time when simply being born a Hebrew meant that Pharaoh was going to choke the life out of you. But Moses got a second chance. He was put in a basket and floated down the Nile River, and God Almighty had the bulrushes grow in the right place to stop that basket with him nestled safely inside. And in just the nick of time, Pharaoh's daughter decided to go down to the river, where she heard baby Moses crying, picked him up out of the bulrushes, and took him to her house where he became the son of the daughter of Pharaoh—the very man who determined to take his life now commanded his daughter to give him life. Years later, Moses killed an Egyptian and was banished from the kingdom. But forty years after that, God found him on the backside of the desert and raised him up to be the great deliverer of His people who had been born in bondage.

David, the sweet psalmist of Israel, walked out on his balcony and saw Bathsheba bathing. He saw that she was beautiful. Then to satisfy his lust, he sent her husband, Uriah the Hittite, to the front line of battle where he was killed. And yet, in the depths of the darkness and depravity of his own despair, David went to God and confessed his sin. God pulled him up out of that mess, and he remained on his kingly throne. And out of his lineage came the Messiah—the Lord Jesus Christ.

Jonah was instructed by God to go to Nineveh to deliver a message of repentance to the people there. Instead, Jonah got on a boat and set sail for Tarshish, which was the opposite direction of Nineveh. But God got Jonah's attention! A great storm arose, and he was thrown overboard where a great whale swallowed him, then deposited him on the shore of Nineveh after three days to fulfill what the Lord had originally instructed him to do. As a result, the king of Nineveh called for repentance and a powerful revival broke out in the land.

What about the woman at the well in Samaria? Jesus told her,

"You've had five husbands, and the one you're with now is not your husband." She begged Him to give her living water, and He did. She had gone to the well looking for natural water and went back to her village with living water, and became the first woman evangelist in the New Testament!

Remember Peter? He denied His master three times before sunrise, as Jesus predicted, as he warmed himself by the fire and feared being discovered as a follower of Jesus. But that same Peter, at the birth of the infant church, stood up and preached the first evangelistic crusade where three thousand men gave their lives to Jesus.

Our precious Lord, the Lamb of God, on that cruel, mean, biting cross turned to the thief, who begged Him to remember him when He came into His kingdom, and replied to him, "Today, you shall be with Me in paradise."

You see, it doesn't matter what you've done, "Jehovah Postscript" is the God of a second chance as He proved Himself to those Israelite men so many years ago who complained they were unable to participate in Passover. God's will for all of us is to be redeemed by the blood of His Son, to walk in His grace, and experience His overwhelming love by giving us a second chance!

Chapter 6

A SEASON OF OUR
LIBERATION AND DELIVERANCE

Therefore if the Son sets you free, you shall be free indeed.
JOHN 8:36

T HE DAY OF PASSOVER HAS FINISHED; ONE MEAL HAS BEEN
consumed, one day of deliverance celebrated, whose meaning
will radiate throughout the coming year. Now it is time for the
Feast of Unleavened Bread to begin!

This Feast of Unleavened Bread, called *Chag HaMatzot* in
Hebrew, is not a joyous celebration though. It is an observance,
a weeklong time of sanctification, also referred to as a season of
liberation by the Jewish people. It is a festival devoted entirely to
the spiritual removal of sin. Sounds a bit heavy, doesn't it? But
when you think of it, sin is a heavy burden.

Beginning with the very first Feast of Passover in the desert,
God set out to illustrate to His people just how serious He was
about removing sin from their lives. At the same time that He gave
Moses instructions for the first Passover, while Israel was still in
Egypt, God gave instructions for the Feast of Unleavened Bread:

> You shall observe the Feast of Unleavened Bread. For on this very day I brought your armies out of the land of Egypt. Therefore you shall observe this day throughout your generations as an ordinance forever. In the first month, on the fourteenth day of the month at evening, you shall eat unleavened bread until the twenty-first day of the month at evening. Seven days shall there be no leaven found in your houses, for whoever eats that which is leavened, that person shall be cut off from the congregation of Israel, whether he be a stranger or born in the land. You shall eat nothing leavened. In all your dwellings you shall eat unleavened bread.
>
> —EXODUS 12:17–20

Yeast, or leaven, which in Hebrew is called *chametz* (khah-METZ), is a very good analogy for sin. Yeast goes to work, out of sight, to raise up, to puff up, and to lift itself up. It is a living, breathing thing, with the sole purpose of exalting, and it does so by feeding itself from the organism it invades and then breeding until it controls that organism. This is a perfect metaphor of what sin does in our lives. Sin is the hidden corruption, the undetected cancer that dwells within us as a corrupting force that works unseen and unheard.

Let's go back for a moment and imagine we are in the desert with the Israelites on the first day after the very first Passover. It is early in the morning of the fifteenth of Nisan, and the people of God have just been commanded to eat only bread without yeast, unleavened bread.

> The Egyptians urged the people, so that they might send them out of the land in haste, for they said, "We all will be dead." So the people took their dough before it was leavened, with their kneading troughs being bound up in their clothes on their shoulders.
>
> —EXODUS 12:33–34

Can you imagine the scene? Two or three million people marching out of Egypt, carrying unleavened dough in their hands, and kneading bowls bound up in their clothes and bags. The lesson is so clear: none of the leaven of Egypt was to go with the Jews to their Promised Land. God did not want to merely remove the Hebrews from Egypt. He wanted to remove the spirit and practices of Egypt—the sinful ways of Egypt—from the hearts of His people.

We can almost hear the ancient words of Isaiah ringing in our ears, as we picture the Israelites leaving Egypt with their bread and their bread bowls in their hands:

> Depart, depart, go out from there, touch no unclean thing; go out of the midst of her; be clean, you who bear the vessels of the LORD.
> —ISAIAH 52:11

The emphasis from God to His chosen people was one of total separation from Egypt. To use another biblical metaphor, it is as though the people of God were to "shake the dust" of Egypt off themselves, as though they are to have not even the tiniest spore of yeast among them that could one day lead to corruption and destruction.

Listen to the terms God uses to explain His feast and command what should be taught regarding it to the next generation:

> You shall observe the Feast of Unleavened Bread. For on this very day I brought your armies out of the land of Egypt.
> —EXODUS 12:17

> Unleavened bread shall be eaten seven days. And there shall be no leavened bread seen among you, nor shall there be leaven seen among you in all your borders. You shall declare to your son on that day, saying, "This is done because of that

which the LORD did for me when I came forth out of Egypt." It shall be as a sign to you on your hand and as a memorial on your forehead, in order that the LORD's law may be in your mouth. For with a strong hand the LORD brought you out of Egypt.

—EXODUS 13:7–9

The Feast of Unleavened Bread has imprinted God's lessons on the hearts of His people through the centuries. In keeping with Jewish tradition, the entire month before Passover is used to remove all leaven from every home. During the weeks prior to Passover, Jewish families will use the Internet and other methods to sell anything they own that has leaven in it. When the feast begins on the day after Passover, homes swept clean of leaven serve only unleavened bread or matzo. Throughout the week no work is done and burnt sacrifices are offered.

THE PURE BREAD OF JESUS CHRIST

The powerful meaning of this Feast of Unleavened Bread was often on the Apostle Paul's mind when he urged the fledgling Christian church to holiness. You will remember, the early church was largely Jewish. Paul's audience in the church in Corinth would have known what he was referring to when he wrote, "Your boasting is not good. Do you not know that a little yeast leavens the whole batch?" (1 Corinthians 5:6).

Most of the young Christians who heard these words from Paul would have observed Passover and the Feast of Unleavened Bread their whole lives. When Paul warned them about a little leaven permeating the whole lump, nearly every member of the New Testament church knew the power of what he said.

Since birth they had eaten the Passover meal of matzo bread without yeast. From childhood they had participated in the search for leaven in their homes, in preparation for a week in which there could be no yeast in any form in their lives.

But Paul's words to the early church regarding unleavened bread had new meaning for those new covenant believers. He was not urging them to feast on unleavened bread. Paul was inviting the church to eat the pure bread of Jesus Christ.

> Therefore purge out the old yeast, that you may be a new batch, since you are unleavened. For even Christ, our Passover, has been sacrificed for us. Therefore let us keep the feast, not with old yeast, nor with the yeast of malice and wickedness, but with the unleavened bread of sincerity and truth.
> —1 CORINTHIANS 5:7–8

Paul was teaching his largely Jewish audience in the early church the difference between life under the old covenant, where sin is combated through human effort, and life in the new covenant, where salvation comes by eating the bread of Jesus Christ.

Consider how God went about revealing Jesus as the unleavened bread of heaven, the fulfillment of all references to unleavened bread throughout biblical history. Jesus is described as "the Bread of Life." He was born in Bethlehem, which in Hebrew means "House of Bread," and He often used bread as an image of Himself: "Unless a kernel of wheat falls to the ground..." (John 12:24, NIV). The truth Jesus preached is even called the "Bread of Life."

Even the matzo bread used at Passover and at the Feast of Unleavened Bread alluded to Jesus with its striped appearance and series of holes—"By his stripes we are healed" (Isaiah 53:5); "They shall look on him whom they pierced" (John 19:37).

What happens when God's people eat the pure bread of Jesus and keep their lives free of the hidden corruption of sin? I'll tell you what happens—victory! Absolute, miraculous victory in God!

As the people of God in Egypt swept their homes clean of leaven and ate only unleavened bread, God delivered them from the hands of their oppressors. It was while they made themselves clean that God acted on their behalf. It was on the very first day of the Feast of Unleavened Bread, the fifteenth of Nisan, that they rose up and left Egypt.

It could be easy to conclude that the first Feast of Unleavened Bread was a bit boring; a week in which God's people just didn't eat a certain kind of bread. Not too exciting, some would say. But in reality it was anything but boring. It was a week of power!

Remember, the Egyptians were so horrified by the deaths of their firstborn that they urged the Hebrews out of the land immediately, even giving them gold and silver and other valuable things. God had changed Pharaoh's heart and provided much needed resources for His people who were poor from years of slavery and oppression. That alone was miraculous. But that's not all that happened during that week.

We know from the writings of the ancient rabbis that it was during the Feast of Unleavened Bread that the Israelites passed through the Red Sea onto dry ground, as they trekked into the wilderness of Sinai. Hot on their heels came the Egyptian army, but as they reached the shores of the Red Sea and plunged forward in pursuit, the waters that had parted for the Israelites rose over them and destroyed them all.

Do you see the power? The Feast of Unleavened Bread is not just a wimpy week of eating light. No! It is a time when God's people remove all evil from their lives and then stand fast to see the salvation of God. Think of it: during that first Feast of Unleavened Bread, the Israelites left 430 years of bondage, with arms full of wealth, marched through barriers that God removed, and then saw their enemies destroyed before their eyes. This is the power of the Feast of Unleavened Bread!

This is what it means to clean out the old leaven and to eat the unleavened bread of sincerity and truth. This is how God responds to a people who make themselves clean before Him. This is how God's people prepare themselves for the victories that God destines for them!

When I think of this powerful feast, I'm reminded of the words of the Apostle Peter in Acts. Standing at one of the gates to the temple in Jerusalem, having just healed a lame man, Peter turned to his mostly Jewish audience and said, "Therefore repent and be converted, that your sins may be wiped away, that times of refreshing may come from the presence of the Lord" (Acts 3:19).

The same themes that are in the Feast of Unleavened Bread are in this verse. If we will repent and turn to God, removing sin from our lives, then God will do magnificent things for us.

It will help you to understand the power of this promise if you know that the Greek word for "refreshing" does not just refer to a bit of inspiration or energy. It doesn't just mean a little bit of encouragement. It is a legal term used in Greek and Roman courts of law that means "the restoration of what has been stolen." Jesus Christ has restored what was stolen from us.

When we repent and remove the leaven of sin from our lives and turn to God, restoration begins. The power of the promise in the Feast of Unleavened Bread sets us free, destroys our enemies, prospers us, and sets our feet on God's path of destiny so that we can "stand, and observe the deliverance of the Lord" (2 Chronicles 20:17).

Chapter 7

DEAD THINGS CAN LIVE AGAIN

Christ has indeed been raised from the dead, the firstfruits of those who have fallen asleep. For since death came through a man, the resurrection of the dead comes also through a man. For as in Adam all die, so in Christ all will be made alive.

1 CORINTHIANS 15:20–22

THE FEAST OF FIRSTFRUITS IS AN EXCITING FESTIVAL; A celebration that took place only after the people of God entered the Promised Land. As they began to prosper in their new land, God wanted them to take the first of their harvest and offer it to Him.

The theme of victory we see in the celebration of the Feast of Unleavened Bread continues in the Feast of Firstfruits, the third of the three feasts that are part of the Passover celebration. In Hebrew it is called *Reishit Katzir* or "the beginning of the harvest."

This feast was unique for many reasons, and one of the most important is that it took place on the first day of the week on the Jewish calendar. God told Moses that this feast should be celebrated on the day after the Sabbath (Saturday) that occurred during the Feast of Unleavened Bread. Since the Feast of Unleavened Bread lasted a week, one of the seven days of that feast was sure to be a Sabbath. This means that Firstfruits has always fallen and will always fall on a Sunday.

Let's consider God's instructions for this feast:

> The LORD spoke to Moses, saying: Speak to the children of Israel, and say to them: When you have come into the land that I am giving to you and reap its harvest, then you shall bring a sheaf bundle of the first fruits of your harvest to the priest. And he shall wave the sheaf before the LORD so that you may be accepted. On the day after the Sabbath the priest shall wave it. You shall offer that day when you wave the sheaf a year-old male lamb without blemish for a burnt offering to the LORD. The grain offering shall be two-tenths of an ephah of wheat flour mixed with oil, a food offering made by fire to the LORD for a pleasing aroma; its drink offering shall be of wine, a fourth of a hin. You shall eat neither bread nor grain, parched or fresh, until the same day that you have brought an offering to your God. It shall be a perpetual statute throughout your generations in all your dwellings.
>
> —LEVITICUS 23:9–14

God had given His people a rich and fertile land. He established the Feast of the Firstfruits as a sacred *mo'edim* so that they could celebrate the richness of His provision for them.

They were instructed to take the very first grain of their harvest, which most likely was a sheaf of barely since barley was the first of the grain crops to ripen, and bring it to a priest. They were not to harvest anything or consume anything until this firstfruit of their harvest had been offered to God. This first sheaf of grain is called an *omer* (OH-mer) in Hebrew.

The priest would wave the grain offering to the north, south, east, and west as a blessing of the harvest and the land. Then a lamb without blemish would be sacrificed before the Lord. All of these actions had symbolic meaning. Through these actions, the people were blessing the land as they gave thanks by declaring, "May this blessing continue. May this bounty continue throughout the land. May this land continue to grant a great harvest for generations to come."

What a thrilling moment that must have been for God's people! After so much torment and so many years of oppression, they are at last in their own land, harvesting its great abundance and giving thanks to God for everything.

We find a deeper understanding of God's will for this firstfruits feast as we read the words that God gave Moses. In this restatement of the commandments for the Feast of Firstfruits, God describes a confession that His people should make, one that honors God and reminds the people of what He has done:

> When you have entered the land the LORD your God is giving you as an inheritance and have taken possession of it and settled in it, take some of the firstfruits of all that you produce from the soil of the land the LORD your God is giving you and put them in a basket.
>
> Then go to the place the LORD your God will choose as a dwelling for his Name and say to the priest in office at the time, "I declare today to the LORD your God that I have come to the land the LORD swore to our ancestors to give us." The priest shall take the basket from your hands and set it down in front of the altar of the LORD your God.
>
> Then you shall declare before the LORD your God: "My father was a wandering Aramean, and he went down into Egypt with a few people and lived there and became a great nation, powerful and numerous. But the Egyptians mistreated us and made us suffer, subjecting us to harsh labor. Then we cried out to the LORD, the God of our ancestors, and the LORD heard our voice and saw our misery, toil and

oppression. So the LORD brought us out of Egypt with a mighty hand and an outstretched arm, with great terror and with signs and wonders.

"He brought us to this place and gave us this land, a land flowing with milk and honey; and now I bring the firstfruits of the soil that you, LORD, have given me." Place the basket before the LORD your God and bow down before him. Then you and the Levites and the foreigners residing among you shall rejoice in all the good things the LORD your God has given to you and your household.

—DEUTERONOMY 26:1–11, NIV

COME, LORD JESUS!

Can you see the unity in the three spring feasts we have just studied? The Feast of Passover is the celebration of redemption. God "passed over" the houses of the Hebrews in Egypt and set His people free. The Feast of Unleavened Bread is a remembrance of the call to be free of sin, and a celebration of the deliverance that comes to God's holy people, who were delivered out of the hands of their oppressors. The Feast of Firstfruits is an offering to God for His abundant provision for His people, who He led into a rich promised land flowing with milk and honey (Exodus 3:8).

The unity of these three festivals has abundant significance to the church today. When you look at the Passion Week, you see that Jesus celebrated each of these three feasts during that week. The Crucifixion took place on Passover, when the blood of the Lamb of God was sacrificed once and for all. Jesus, who is without sin, was buried on the day of the Feast of Unleavened Bread. And on the feast of Firstfruits our Lord and Savior was raised from the dead—the firstfruits of those who have died.

Let's look more closely at the progression of the Passion Week, Jesus's final week on Earth.

- **Nisan 14:** We know that this is the date of the Jewish Passover, and we know that Jesus celebrated His Passover meal or *Seder* on this night with His disciples.

- **Nisan 15:** This was the Sabbath, and on this day Jesus lay in the tomb. Since this is the day after Passover, it was also the first day of the Feast of Unleavened Bread.

- **Nisan 16:** Jesus was raised from the dead, on the Sunday after the Sabbath during the Feast of the Unleavened Bread.

I find this truth to be thrilling—that Jesus was raised from the dead on the Feast of Firstfruits. Listen to what Paul said about it:

> Christ has indeed been raised from the dead, the firstfruits of those who have fallen asleep. For since death came through a man, the resurrection of the dead comes also through a man.
>
> For as in Adam all die, so in Christ all will be made alive. But each in turn: Christ, the firstfruits; then, when he comes, those who belong to him.
>
> —1 CORINTHIANS 15:20–23, NIV

Imagine if you can, the scene that likely unfolded on the day Jesus was raised from the dead. It is Sunday, the first day of the week. The Sabbath day was the day before, during the Feast of Unleavened Bread. It was also the Sabbath immediately after Passover.

Now, on this Sunday morning, the women who were among the disciples of Jesus rushed to the tomb where He was buried. Normally, they would have anointed His body with spices and oils on Friday, when He was buried, but they were unable because the sun was setting. They could not return on Saturday to complete their task because it was the Sabbath. Now, on Sunday morning, they have important work to do. They must prepare the body with the spices and fragrant oils they are carrying before any more time goes by.

As they hurry to the grave, smoke ascends from the temple; an unblemished lamb is being sacrificed. This is the special sacrifice for the Feast of Firstfruits. The priests at the temple are doing what priests have done on this day for generations.

Finally the women arrive at the garden tomb only to discover to their dismay that Jesus is not there. "He has risen," they are told. These dear women had no way of knowing at that moment, but the most significant event in the history of mankind had occurred. Jesus Christ, the Lamb of God, had become the Firstfruit for all mankind.

Through Him, God has delivered all who are willing to believe. The curtain has been torn in two, from top to bottom; the veil separating mankind from God has been removed, bringing all believers into the rich and abundant promised land of the kingdom of God. "Alleluia. Christ our Passover is sacrificed for us. Therefore, let us keep the feast! Alleluia!"[1]

This is good news for me and you. Your years of oppression and rebellious wandering have ended. Now you can begin to enjoy the seed time, and the harvest time in the kingdom of God. You can begin to reap the glorious riches that have been provided by our Lord.

We must never forget that Firstfruits means that we ought always to live in gratitude, in heartfelt acknowledgment of God's grace and in humble recognition that we were lost but now we are found. God has delivered us, planted us, and set our feet upon His path of an abundant life in Jesus.

Before we end our study of the Passion Week, there is one other event from that week worth contemplation. Matthew

27:50–53 tells us: "And Jesus, when He had cried out again with a loud voice, released His spirit. At that moment the curtain of the temple was torn in two, from the top to the bottom. And the ground shook, and the rocks split apart. The graves also were opened, and many bodies of the saints who had died were raised, and coming out of the graves after His resurrection, they went into the Holy City and appeared to many."

Did you catch that? "The tombs broke open and the bodies of many holy people who had died were raised to life." It is as if, immediately after Jesus died on the cross, He offered up a firstfruits offering to God as a foretaste of the great harvest of souls that is to come!

What does this Feast of Firstfruits mean to you? To me, it means that in Jesus Christ, as a result of His abundant grace in my life through faith, I have entered into my Promised Land. And if this is true for me, it is true for you also. Hear this: Jesus Christ is your Promised Land! Don't wait another minute. Receive what God has for you now!

Chapter 8

HOLY SPIRIT, COME!

Apart from the spirit of God we can do nothing. We are ships without the wind or chariots without steeds to pull them; like branches without sap, we are withered.[1]

CHARLES H. SPURGEON

ENTECOST, THE FOURTH FEAST OF THE SEVEN MAJOR feasts of God, is also known by several other names. In Hebrew, it is called *Shavuot* (sha-voo-OHT), which means "weeks." As a result, you will often hear Pentecost referred to as "the Feast of Weeks," yet you know it better as "the Feast of Pentecost."

Many of our Jewish friends use another name for this feast: *Atzeret Pesach* (aht-ZEH-reht PAY-sahk), which means "Conclusion of Passover." Even though the Feast of Weeks is not one of the three feasts most associated with Passover, it marks the conclusion of Passover, the first "stage" in the creation of a people of God.

On Shavuot, the prescribed offering was in the form of two loaves of bread (not unleavened bread). During the time of the temple in Jerusalem, Shavuot was celebrated by a pilgrimage to the temple, where the loaves would be offered to the temple priests.

But the Feast of Weeks is more than another celebration of a rich harvest. According to rabbinic tradition, the Feast of Weeks occurred on the same day of the year that Moses gave the Torah to the people in the desert. "In the third month after the children of Israel had gone out of the land of Egypt, on the same day, they came to the Wilderness of Sinai" (Exodus 19:1, NKJV).

So, Israel left Egypt on the fifteenth day of the first month. Forty-five days later the people arrived at Mount Sinai. Moses went up the holy mountain for one day, and three days of preparation followed. At the conclusion of these three days, the covenant was sealed in blood. The people went up the mountain with Moses to meet with God. When you do the math, this is fifty days in all. This was the great moment the Torah was revealed, a day seared into the heart of every Hebrew man and woman. God had given His chosen people His revelation.

Just as Shavuot celebrated the end of the harvest season over a period of forty-nine days, leading up to day fifty—so we see this pattern of days reflected in the giving of the Torah to the people of God. Indeed, our God is a God of times and dates, of symbols and patterns. He wanted His people to celebrate the latter part of the harvest, but He also wanted them to remember the giving of the Torah and to celebrate it as well.

In Leviticus 23 the Magna Carta chapter of the feasts of God, the commandments regarding this Feast of Weeks are very specific:

> From the day after the Sabbath, the day you brought the sheaf of the wave offering, count off seven full weeks. Count off fifty days up to the day after the seventh Sabbath, and then present an offering of new grain to the LORD.
>
> From where you live, bring two loaves made of two-tenths of an ephah of the finest flour, baked with yeast, as a wave offering of firstfruits to the LORD.
>
> Present with this bread with seven male lambs, each a year old and without defect, one young bull and two rams. They will be a burnt offering to the LORD, together with

their grain offerings and drink offerings—a food offering, an aroma pleasing to the LORD. Then sacrifice one male goat for a sin offering and two lambs, each a year old, for a fellowship offering. The priest is to wave the two lambs before the LORD as a wave offering, together with the bread of the firstfruits. They are a sacred offering to the LORD for the priest.

On that same day, you are to proclaim a sacred assembly and do no regular work. This is to be a lasting ordinance for the generations to come, wherever you live. When you reap the harvest of your land, do not reap to the very edges of your field or gather the gleanings of your harvest. Leave them for the poor and for the foreigner residing among you. I am the LORD your God.

—LEVITICUS 23:15–22, NIV

God makes it clear that He wants this fourth feast to take place exactly fifty days or seven weeks and a day after the Feast of Firstfruits.

It's interesting to note, the word *Pentecost* by which we Christians usually refer to this festival, is the Greek word for "fiftieth day." So, both the Greek and the Hebrew words for this festival come from the period of time—fifty days or seven weeks and a day—between the Feast of Firstfruits and the Feast of Weeks.

THE COUNTING OF THE OMER

So significant is this forty-nine-day gap between these two feasts, that Jewish tradition has given it a name and a ceremony: *Sefirat HaOmer* (SEH-fih-raht hah-OH-mer) in Hebrew, or the "Counting of the Omer." Remember, *omer* means "sheaf." So on each day of the forty-nine days between these two feasts the sheaves of grain were counted and celebrated. The joy of this grand celebration of the bounty of the Lord was much like an extension of the joy that attended the Feast of Firstfruits.

Each evening after the omers were counted but before the number was announced, the chief rabbi would recite the following blessing:

> Blessed are you, O Lord our God, King of the universe, Who by His command to count the omer has sanctified us.

Next, Jewish tradition required Psalm 67 to be recited. Is it surprising that Psalm 67 is composed of exactly forty-nine Hebrew words, the same as the number of days ordained for counting the omer? I think not!

> May God be gracious to us, and bless us,
>> and cause His face to shine on us; Selah
>> that Your way may be known on earth,
>> Your salvation among all nations.
> Let the peoples praise You, O God;
>> let all the peoples praise You.
> Oh, let the nations be glad and sing for joy;
>> for You will judge the people uprightly,
>> and lead the nations on earth. Selah
> Let the peoples praise You, O God;
>> let all the peoples praise You.
> Then will the earth yield its produce,
>> and God, our God, will bless us.
> God will bless us,
>> and all the ends of the earth will fear Him.

TO REDEEM THE WHOLE EARTH

Now, there is another meaning to this great Feast of Pentecost. Did you by any chance catch it when you read Leviticus 23? Remember, God commanded that the two loaves that were to be waved before the Lord were to be made *with* leaven. God purposely left out the aspect of sin in this holy festival. But why? What was He saying to His people?

You will recall that in the latter part of the harvest of Israel, God desired that His people remember the outsiders. By leaving the leaven in the bread offering, He was reminding His people that the Gentiles—those "leavened" ones who were outside "unleavened" Israel—were going to be welcomed too.

What good news this is for you and for me! These two loaves symbolize the very reason that you and I are in Christ, in the church of Jesus, and in the kingdom of God. These two loaves represent sinful mankind. They represent men with the sinful nature "baked" in them. But God has mercy on sinners! He has made a way for everyone to come to Him, through Jesus.

Look at this commandment at the end of all God's instructions for the Feast of Weeks.

> When you reap the harvest of your land, you shall not reap up to the edge of your field....Leave them for the poor and stranger: I am the LORD your God.
> —LEVITICUS 19:9–10

God is not just thinking of His chosen people. His heart is turned toward everyone, the great unwashed majority of humanity, because He desires that not one should perish (2 Peter 3:9).

Can you hear Him speaking to His people, telling them, "Remember the Gentiles. Remember that you are blessed to be a blessing. Remember that I intend to redeem the whole earth, not just Israel. Don't forget them, rich and poor, in all that you do, even in how you bring in the harvests I give you."

THE PROMISE FULFILLED

God cared for the wider world outside of Israel, and if there was ever a day that fulfilled this divine concern, it was the Day of

Pentecost. The Greek name, Pentecost, means "fifty," referring to the fifty days after the Feast of Firstfruits on which Pentecost occurred.

On that fiftieth day, according to Acts 1:4–8, the disciples had been commanded not to depart from Jerusalem, but to wait for the promised "power from on high" that was to be poured out on them. And so, they gathered in Jerusalem, just as Jesus had commanded them to do before He ascended to the Father.

We know from Acts 1:13 that the disciples gathered in an upper room in a house in the city, and there they chose Judas's successor. However, according to Acts 2:1–4 when the Holy Spirit was poured out, He filled them and "the house" where they were assembled. But the tradition of saying the Holy Spirit was poured out "in the upper room" is not supported by the text.

The Holy Spirit was poured out upon many from Gentile nations as specifically listed in the Book of Acts: Parthians, Medes, and Elamites; residents of Mesopotamia, Judea, and Cappadocia, Pontus, Asia, Phrygia, Pamphylia, Egypt, and parts of Libya near Cyrene; visitors from Rome (both Jews and converts to Judaism); Cretans; and Arabians. When you count them, fifteen Gentile lands are mentioned.

Then as Peter begins to address the crowd, explaining to them what has just happened and giving them the good news of the gospel, the Scriptures tell us that many were born again. The fledgling church is beginning to reap a harvest of souls in the power of the Holy Spirit!

Can you think of a greater fulfillment of God's passion for the lost Gentile world than for a new covenant church comprised of every tribe and tongue? Oh, how beautifully and perfectly the Day of Pentecost fulfills the heart of God expressed in the Feast of Weeks. What better fulfillment of the twin symbols of harvest and leavened bread, than a harvest of Gentiles, filled with the

Spirit of the living God, added to the Israelites, the chosen people of God? This is truly the glorious church as God intends it.

How joyfully are those who were "alienated from the citizenship of Israel and strangers to the covenants of promise, without hope and without God in the world" (Ephesians 2:12) can lift up a shout of thanks and praise to God for His great mercy!

Through recognition of God's Feast of Weeks, we can draw a direct line to its historical fulfillment and genesis in the teachings of our Lord regarding the outpouring and infilling of the mighty Holy Spirit that came in Acts 2.

As we conclude this examination of Pentecost, I want to invite you to take an honest look at what the Pentecostal experience means in your life, and in the life of the church today. I believe it is God's great desire that we are and remain an Acts 2 people—expressing the very life of God within us and being led by the precious Holy Spirit on a daily basis.

THE WHITE HOT HEAT
OF THE HOLY SPIRIT

The Pentecostal experience promises power to propel us across that great theological divide between the old and new covenant, so that we may realize that the God in Christ becomes the Christ in us. Just as Jesus showed us the Father, so we now show Jesus to this dying world.

We have a physical body for one reason: to give expression to the life of Christ that is within us. Think of it this way: people enjoy shaking your hand when greeting you, however, if it was severed from your body in an accident, I doubt they would be as interested in shaking it! Our physical bodies were not created to be separated from the life of God within us.

The Spirit of God within us gives us, as individuals and as the church at large, the connection that makes both our natural body and the body of Christ on Earth, alive with vitality, power, and purpose. "We have this treasure in earthen vessels, the excellency of the power being from God and not from ourselves" (2 Corinthians 4:7).

Unfortunately, we live in a time when a powerless Pentecost has become the norm and not the exception, because there is a price to be paid. Though Pentecost meant power to the disciples, it also meant prison to them. Have you noticed that Pentecost means empowerment, but it also brings banishment from organized religion? While Pentecost brings favor with God, it can bring hatred from men. It can bring tremendous miracles and mighty obstacles.

The church today often has more perversion than power, more playboys than prophets, and more compromise than conviction. What we need is the One who condescends to indwell mortals, to fill us full of Himself. We need Him no matter the cost.

A. W. Tozer, one of the great theologians of the twentieth century wrote, "The average Christian is so cold and contented with his wretched condition that there is no vacuum of desire into which the blessed Spirit can rush in satisfying fullness."[2]

Have you noticed that we have to hang a sign outside our church to announce we are Pentecostal, because without a sign, no one could identify us? And sadly, most of the time the sign outside the church is the only "sign" anyone will see. Once inside, they will find placating pastors who are afraid and ashamed to let the power of God have free rein lest someone be offended. Imagine, we are afraid someone will be offended by the presence of God!

Here are those pointed words from the original Pentecostal prophet Joel:

> It will be that, afterwards, I will pour out My Spirit on all flesh; then your sons and your daughters will prophesy,

your old men will dream dreams, and your young men will
see visions.

—JOEL 2:28

The Apostle Peter said the holy angels of God would desire to understand this mystery (1 Peter 1:12). Zechariah said it would fall like rain (Zechariah 10:1), and Amos said it would take some preparation (Amos 4:7). Hosea preached that it would require the breaking up of our fallow ground (Hosea 10:12). But I love the picture that Malachi painted: suddenly He will come to His temple (Malachi 3:1)!

We need another drenching downpour of Pentecostal power. We have no power in public, because we don't pray in tongues in private. We are void of an earthly word, because we are empty of heaven's language.

Should we be content with a shout in the sanctuary, but no clout in the spirit or with authority that takes no meaningful ground? No! Why write songs of victory over evil that are more suitable for the playground than the battleground? Have we become so proficient in the dialect of men that we are empty of the voice of heaven?

Between the harshness and the humor of this litany of the powerless Pentecostal is the truth of the church today. We have become so complacent on the outer fringes of His works that we have forgotten the inner essence of His power.

Many who claim to have experienced the baptism of the Holy Ghost are more dead than alive, more spirit-frilled than Spirit-filled. Because whenever evil mires the work of God, our flesh reasserts itself. Our lack of fruit exposes our prayerless, power-less, and passionless Christianity. As harsh as all of this sounds, let it be exhortation to your spirit rather than condemnation.

On the Day of Pentecost, Peter prayed ten days and then

preached ten minutes. Now we pray ten minutes, and preach ten days, and wonder why we have so many failures.

Let's become a people of God who are ready to lose our dignity for a demonstration. Are you ready to repent, even if it means your reputation? Will you take a chance and forego marketing for miracles? How about laying aside tongues of poison for tongues of fire? "Now the Spirit speaketh expressly, that in the latter times some shall depart from the faith, giving heed to seducing spirits, and doctrines of devils" (1 Timothy 4:1, KJV). Let's stop being ashamed of the "full" gospel.

Context is important. If you're enjoying a good movie at a theater and shout "fire!" the authorities will lock you up. However, we need some preachers and believers in the church, in this hour, to shout "Fire!"—"Holy Ghost fire"—if we are to see multitudes saved, healed, and delivered.

The apostate church will continue its cold indifference to a true move of God's Holy Spirit in the earth even, as the true apostolic church continues to grows to maturity and prepare the earth for the imminent return of our Lord and Savior, Jesus Christ.

> "Who among us can live with the continual fire? Who among us can live with everlasting burning?" He who walks righteously and speaks uprightly…
> —ISAIAH 33:14–15

God Almighty desires to permanently remove from your life anything you don't want and everything you don't need by your surrendering them to Him and exposing them to the white hot heat of the Holy Spirit. This devouring fire of the presence of God is available to you and to me. Oh, that His glory would annihilate everything in our lives that would hinder His full blessing from resting upon us.

May we all plead to burn off the dross: "Oh, blessed Holy

Spirit, make me by Your fire pure and clean." And in the words of Zechariah 14:20, "Holy to the Lord."

I want to share with you a prophetic word of both warning and encouragement:

> You have been set on a collision course with your adversary, the devil. Know that you were built for the battle and created for the conflict. Your armor prophesies warfare, and your enemy is about to encounter a God with whom he cannot contend, nor can he fence in nor flee from. The God who has heretofore been fighting with you is about to fight for you!

God desires a holy people, set apart for Him, to help bring His kingdom to Earth, but who will yield completely to Him, surrendering to the power of the Holy Spirit?

Fire can burn up and it can also amalgamate, which means to join two as one in a permanent state. Our prayer must become such that we are so melted by the baptism of Pentecostal fire, that those areas of inconsistency and fluctuation in our devotion to Christ and our influence upon this generation are fused together in the steadfast consistency of His Spirit.

It is here that we will see the fulfillment of the high priestly prayer of our Lord in John 17:21, "That they may all be one, as You, Father, are in Me, and I in You. May they also be one in Us, that the world may believe that You have sent Me."

Luke 3:16 promises that the Lord Jesus Christ will baptize us in fire. I believe we can be so totally immersed in God that we become peace, joy, hope, and healing, as we die in the fiery ocean of His presence, and resurrect in the permanence and consistency of His character. May we pray for permanent faith, permanent joy, permanent peace, abiding commitment, and Christ-like character!

BLESSINGS OF
OBEDIENCE AT PENTECOST

Your Bible reveals an often overlooked but vital truth in the very beginning of the Book of Acts. In Acts 1:4–5 Jesus gave this unqualified instruction to His followers: He "commanded that they should not depart from Jerusalem, but wait for the promise of the Father…for John truly baptized with water; but you shall be baptized with the Holy Ghost not many days hence." Bible scholars tell us there were likely five hundred people who heard that command from the mouth of the risen Savior, but Acts 1:13 tells us that only one hundred twenty were present on that day. From five hundred down to one hundred twenty—only one-fourth obeyed the command and received the blessing. The other three-fourths of the people missed their opportunity to receive the destiny-altering, life-transforming power that was released, simply because they didn't obey the instruction.

1. Power

The first blessing of Pentecost is power. This power isn't transient. You don't have it, then lose it. It doesn't run out. Because the power of Pentecost extends from time immortal, down through the ages and continues on today to the end of the age when Jesus returns for His church. It is perpetually regenerating itself. That is because it comes from God Himself who is and was and will forever be. That power is capable of overcoming every problem, sickness, and stronghold in your life. Paul wrote, "For God has not given us the spirit of fear, but of power, and love, and self-control" (2 Timothy 1:7).

Your fear isn't simply an emotional response. Fear and faith are mutually exclusive and diametrically opposed. They can't live in the same heart or the same mind. One cancels out the other. That's why Mark 11:22 says: "Have faith in God." The power, love and sound mind you have aren't simply mental attributes. You have them by and through the Spirit of the living God.

2. Peace

The second blessing is peace. Paul refers to it this way: "And the peace of God, which surpasses all understanding, will protect your hearts and minds through Christ Jesus" (Philippians 4:7). The Pentecost peace that God has imparted to you through the Holy Spirit "surpasses" all of your understanding.

That means you might be thinking about something one way and see your utter limitation in light of it. In fact, it might appear that there's no light at all and you're wandering around lost in darkness. The peace that God provides is the light in that dark cavern. Here's the good news, you can have the peace of God, regardless of your circumstances. In fact, the Pentecost blessing of peace operates regardless of the situation. In the face of any conflict, large or small, you can have peace.

3. Protection

The third blessing God desires to release during Pentecost season is protection. The Bible says God will give His angels charge concerning you. You're surrounded by heavenly forces, God's body guards, if you will. But God doesn't only protect you by these angelic forces. His protection also comes from the inside out through the Holy Spirit. The Bible refers to this as the "still, small voice" of God (1 Kings 19:12).

So if you find yourself in an overwhelming situation, God can send angels to protect you or He can speak to you through the Holy Spirit, guiding you to avoid a bad situation in the first place. Let me tell you, I'm so thankful for God's protection in times of trouble, but if He'll help me avoid the problem in the first place, it's so much better! This is what the Holy Spirit can and will do. When you find yourself bumping up against an unsolvable situation, the very best thing you can do is pray in the Spirit, which is letting the Holy Spirit pray through you!

4. Presence

The fourth blessing of Pentecost is God's presence. The presence of the Lord is steadfast, new every morning, and it never, ever changes. More than anything else, you need the manifested presence of Almighty God upon your life. In His presence there really is fullness of joy and it's where everything you need comes to full fruition and glorious manifestation. David, the sweet psalmist of Israel said, "My soul longs, yes, even faints for the courts of the LORD; my heart and my body cry out for the living God....For a day in Your courts is better than a thousand elsewhere" (Psalm 84:2, 10).

5. Prosperity

The fifth blessing of Pentecost is prosperity. Oh, how God desires to bless us! Our Bible says He delights in the prosperity of His servants! His blessings are so great, so extravagant. They're always spoken of in the Bible in the most amplified, larger-than-life terms. The prophet Malachi said God "will...open for you the windows of heaven and pour out for you a blessing, that there will not be room enough to receive it" (Malachi 3:10). Jesus said, "Give, and it will be given to you: Good measure, pressed down, shaken together, and running over will men give unto you" (Luke 6:38).

God's prosperity always exceeds our boundaries. We might be thinking and asking, "God, if You could just fill up this little basket or room that I have, I'd be content." Yet God says, "Your basket and room are too small. I'm going to give you 'more than you could ask or think.'" Isaiah 54:2 shouts it: "Enlarge the place of your tent, and let them stretch out the curtains of your habitations; spare not, lengthen your cords, and strengthen your stakes."

It's time to take the limits off God, because the prosperity that God desires to release into your life is far greater than anything you could ever think or imagine. It's limitless!

All five of these blessings were released into the life of King David and his son Solomon. A plague had swept over the land, and David's people were perishing by the thousands. He desperately needed a miracle. God spoke to him to make a sacrificial offering on a particular threshing floor. The owner wanted to give it to King David, but David refused, saying, "I will not offer up to the LORD burnt offerings that cost me nothing" (2 Samuel 24:24). King David paid the owner fifty silver shekels. Fifty—the number associated with Pentecost! It was an extravagant amount of money by any standard. When he did, supernatural healing swept through the land and the outpouring of the blessing of God was released.

I pray for the manifestation of each one of these Pentecost blessings in your life as you obey God's every command in His great desire to bless you through the gift of His precious Holy Spirit.

PART THREE

CELEBRATING
THE END
OF THE AGE

Chapter 9

STARTING OVER

Listen, I tell you a mystery: We shall not all sleep, but we shall all be changed. In a moment, in the twinkling of an eye, at the last trumpet, for the trumpet will sound, the dead will be raised incorruptible, and we shall be changed. For this corruptible will put on incorruption, and this mortal will put on immortality.

1 Corinthians 15:51–53

Before we begin to fully explore the Feast of Trumpets, allow me to first remind you that the fall festivals in the Hebrew calendar start in Tishrei, which is September in our Gregorian calendar. If you recall, the first three feasts of God occurred in the first month of the Hebrew calendar, Nisan, which is approximately April in our Gregorian calendar. Pentecost occurs in late May or early June. So the fall feasts are quite a jump in time from the Feast of Pentecost! This vast leap in time parallels a vast leap in the emphases of the feasts.

While the spring feasts of God were about redemption, deliverance, God's abundant provision, and the revelation of God given to the Jews, the fall feasts had a heavier tone to them—a tone of awakening, repentance, God's judgment, and ultimately of God making all things new.

There is another great difference between the spring and fall festivals that is important to note. While the spring festivals are fulfilled in the life of Jesus Christ and in the coming of the Holy Spirit on the Day of Pentecost, most Christian teachers believe that the fall festivals are as yet unfulfilled, prophetic statements awaiting the second coming of our Lord Jesus. This is both an exciting and challenging thought, and sometimes one that is difficult to interpret. Come with me now as we work our way through this interpretation.

ROSH HASHANAH—THE FEAST OF TRUMPETS AND AWAKENING TO JUDGMENT

> On Rosh Hashanah, everything we do is imbued with extreme significance. We stand in judgment before the Heavenly Court while each of our actions, words, and thoughts are scrutinized.[1]
>
> —RABBI MOSHE SCHUCHMAN

The first of the fall feasts on the Hebrew calendar is the Feast of Trumpets, which in Hebrew is *Yom Teruah* (yahm tuh-RU-ah), the "day of noise." Jews commonly refer to this feast as *Rosh Hashanah*, which literally means "head of the year." It is the Jewish New Year's Day and is celebrated on the first two days of Tishrei.

> In the seventh month, on the first day of the month, you shall have a sabbath, a memorial with the blowing of trumpets, a holy convocation.
>
> —LEVITICUS 23:24

Rosh Hashanah is sometimes referred to by yet another name— the "Day of Remembrance" or *Yom ha-Zikaron* (yahm ha-ZEE-kah-rahn), on which the shofar is to be blown commemorating the sixth day of creation when God created Adam and Eve.

TEN DAYS OF AWE

Rosh Hashanah begins a ten-day period during which Jews enter into self-examination and repentance, known as the Ten Days of Awe, which conclude on Yom Kippur, the Day of Atonement. During this time, God, in a sense, withdraws His presence in order to create a hunger in the hearts of His people so that they will abandon all else in pursuit of Him.

Whereas God is usually seeking us, during the Ten Days of Awe, we are to seek Him. The prerogative is His. It is as if the Father is saying to His children, "If you want to know Me, seek Me!"

But we cannot seek God unless He first puts that desire in our hearts, and when He does, the responsibility to seek Him becomes ours. David the psalmist said it this way: "My heart says of you, "Seek his face!" Your face, LORD, I will seek" (Psalm 27:8). During the Days of Awe, God desires that we clear the stage of our lives, crush our idols, and in repentance, press into His presence in utter abandoned praise and worship to Him, the glorious King of the universe.

> Yom Kippur is not about personal resolutions and private reflection. It is about standing up and talking to God. It is about apologizing, about reestablishing our connection with our Creator. We must tell God who we are, where we are holding in life, and what we know needs improvement.[2]
>
> —RABBI DOVID ROSENFELD

It is interesting to note that God's directives regarding this period (encompassing Rosh Hashanah, Ten Days of Awe, and Yom Kippur) are quite limited. What little He has to say is found in the Books of Leviticus and Numbers:

The LORD spoke to Moses, saying: Speak to the children of Israel, saying: In the seventh month, on the first day of the month, you shall have a sabbath, a memorial with the blowing of trumpets, a holy convocation. You shall do no regular work, and you shall offer a food offering made by fire to the LORD.

—LEVITICUS 23:23-25

In the seventh month, on the first day of the month, you will have a holy assembly. You will do no ordinary work. It is a day of blowing the trumpets for you. You will offer a burnt offering as a pleasing aroma to the LORD: one young bull, one ram, and seven lambs in their first year, without blemish.

—NUMBERS 29:1–2

Could it be that God is saying much by saying very little? Is He again placing the responsibility on us? While the Scriptures give us little insight, the sages and the Talmud provide significant insight, revealing more about this very sacred period, which was communicated to Moses from Jehovah and passed down orally from generation to generation.

GOD OPENS HIS BOOK

On Rosh Hashanah, God opens the Book of Account. Now don't allow this Book of Account to be a point of confusion for you. Some teach that this book is the same as the Lamb's Book of Life found in the Book of Revelation, but that's not the case.

It's only appropriate to teach on the Book of Life once Jesus established the new covenant. When Jesus made propitiation at Calvary, we entered into the new covenant with eternal life secured through the blood of our spotless Lamb and, if you've received Him as your Savior, your name has been recorded in His Book of Life!

But here, we're studying the old covenant practice where the Book of Account records the righteous or wicked actions of man for one year. So the book is opened and for ten days, God judges from it, then closes or seals it on Yom Kippur for another year, thus sealing the fate of the next year.

The Days of Awe are a time of deep introspection and repentance for the Jewish people. Remember, the first message of John the Baptist was "repent" (Matthew 3:1–2), as was the first message of Jesus Christ (Matthew 4:17).

It is interesting to note that the posture of one's heart during this period of reflection is supposed to mirror the shape of the shofar—a bent shape. Rather than looking straight to God, we are to look at ourselves then earnestly seek His face.

Though we should be in a posture of repentance every day of the year, quick to seek God for forgiveness of our sins, when we know we are about to stand before Him, a special level of repentance and cleansing should occur.

I am so grateful for the access that we have to God through the blood of Jesus. "Let us then come with confidence to the throne of grace, that we may obtain mercy and find grace to help in time of need" (Hebrews 4:16). Yet the Days of Awe remind me that I want to be pure and holy before my God, because it is a "fearful thing to fall into the hands of the living God" (Hebrews 10:31). I want to be part of the bride of Christ who has "made herself ready" for the "wedding of the Lamb" (Revelation 19:7, NIV).

But Rosh Hashanah is not only about commemoration of the sixth day of creation. According to the sages, Rosh Hashanah is also a day for the coronation of our God as King, both on a personal level and national level. A blast from the shofar is meant to jolt the people of God awake, so that they can honor God as the absolute sovereign King of the universe. In the Talmud, God asks for His people to "talk to Him and say before Him that your remembrance comes before Him for good." In other words, declare Him sovereign! Psalm 2:7 says, "I will declare the decree: The LORD has said to Me, 'You are My Son, today I have begotten You'" (NKJV).

THE SHOFAR

> Happy are the people who learn from the Shofar! Shofar wakes, calls the alarm, announces royalty, trumpets victory, signals God's power—and mercy. Shofar recalls the ram whose hidden presence in the bushes saved our beloved father, Isaac.[3]
>
> —MAKOM OHR SHALOM MACHZOR

God seems to like the sound of trumpets, especially the shofar, which is mentioned in the Bible more than any other musical instrument. The shofar, a biblical ram's horn trumpet, is used by the people of God on many occasions for a variety of reasons. The shofar was blown to summon Israel to meet with God in the Book of Exodus (Exodus 19:13). It proclaimed the Year of Jubilee (Leviticus 25:8–10), summoned God's people to repentance (Joel 2:15), and warned of trouble (Joel 2:1). But most impressive of all, the shofar was blown more than one hundred times on Rosh Hashanah, the Feast of Trumpets.

There are those who have suggested that God's love for this biblical ram's horn trumpet came about when Isaac was spared by a ram caught in a thicket by its horn. Their reasoning is that without Isaac there would be no Jews, and without the Jews there would be no Jesus, and of course, without Jesus, there would be no Messiah, apostles, and all that follows.

The blowing of a ram's horn is very important in the life of Israel. In the days leading up to Rosh Hashanah, the shofar is to be blown every day except the Shabbat to awaken God's people for the coming feast. There are four standard blasts that are traditionally used. The first, which is a long single blast signaling the King's coronation, is called the *Tekiah* (te-KEE-ah). It is followed by the *Sheviah* (SHEV-ee-ah), which consists of three short blasts that sound like a human wail, and call God's people to repentance. Next is the *Teru'ah* (tuh-RU-ah), a series of short blasts, like alarms, calling the faithful to awaken. And the *Tekiah haGadol* (te-KEE-ah ha-guh-DOL), which ends the Shofar blessings, is one great blast that lasts as long as the *baal tekiah* (buh-ahl te-KEE-ah)—the shofar virtuoso—has breath to sustain it!

On the Jewish day of the great Feast of Trumpets, a sacred assembly is held. The customary blasts of the shofar call out, summoning the people to remembrance and repentance, and giving the all-important signal, "Awake!" Food is offered to the Lord as a sacrifice, and the people eat together. In more modern times, Jewish people also light candles, eat apples dipped in honey, and enjoy *challah* (KHAH-luh) bread shaped like a crown. Thus begins their literal and symbolic process of repentance.

Prophetic insights lead many to believe that the second coming of Jesus could very well occur on Rosh Hashanah. Nobody knows exactly when Jesus is coming back—it could be years from this moment, or it might be before you turn this page. Listen to what the Apostle Paul wrote about the second coming of Jesus:

> The Lord Himself will descend from heaven with a shout, with the voice of the archangel, and with the trumpet call of God. And the dead in Christ will rise first. Then we who are alive and remain shall be caught up together with them in the clouds to meet the Lord in the air. And so we shall be forever with the Lord.
> —1 THESSALONIANS 4:16–17

One thing is very clear, the last trumpet will sound, and we will rise to be with Jesus! Hallelujah!

Although God can sound the trumpet any time He chooses, He seems to take particular care as to when and for what purpose He uses it. He is the God of details, who knows you by name and numbers the hairs on your head (Matthew 10:30). He plans out prophecy and its fulfillment. He, who established the Feast of Trumpets, will one day return to the sound of a trumpet, and it is entirely possible it could be on the Feast of Trumpets. "Amen. Even so, come Lord Jesus" (Revelation 22:20).

THE ROSH HASHANAH RETREAT

Unlike all other Jewish feasts, Rosh Hashanah and Yom Kippur are not historic in application. They were not established to commemorate significant events in Israel's national history. Rather, they speak to us of immediacy, the here and the now of divine encounter.

As you will recall from our study, the Feast of Passover celebrates the deliverance of God's people from slavery in Egypt. The Feast of Unleavened Bread commemorates the fact that when the Israelites were finally freed from bondage in Egypt, they had to flee so quickly that there was no time to let their bread rise. The Feast of Firstfruits marks the start of the harvest, a time to give God thanks with the firstfruits of the fields. The Feast of Pentecost is based on the Israelite tradition that Moses received the Law on Mount Sinai exactly fifty days after the Feast of Firstfruits. And, the Feast of Tabernacles commemorates the forty-year period following freedom from bondage, when the Israelites lived in temporary shelters during their wilderness experience.

> The *sukkah*, the booth, is the central symbol of the ancient Israelites' trust and hope for forty years in the desert. The

Hebrews left the protection of man-made thick walls to place themselves under the protection of God. Exposed to dangerous natural conditions and hostile roving bands, they placed their confidence in the divine concern, which is the only true source of security.[4]

—RABBI IRVING GREENBERG

During this period of what I like to call the "Rosh Hashanah retreat," I'm always mindful of the story of Jesus calming the storm from the Gospel of Mark.

> That same day, when the evening came, He said to them, "Let us go cross to the other side." When they had sent the crowd away, they took Him in the boat just as He was. There were also other little boats with Him. A great wind storm arose, and the waves splashed into the boat, so that it was now filling the boat. He was in the stern asleep on a pillow. They woke Him and said, "Teacher, do You not care that we are perishing?"
>
> He rose and rebuked the wind, and said to the sea, "Peace, be still!" Then the wind ceased and there was a great calm.
>
> —MARK 4:35–39

You'll notice that Jesus had withdrawn. In fact, He was at rest, asleep. Remember, on Rosh Hashanah the Jews are to blow the shofar to awaken them from their sleep so that they can honor God. When a person sleeps, they are not "gone, or dead." They simply are not manifesting their presence outwardly or externally. The fact that Jesus was asleep in the boat caused His followers to seek Him, find Him, and awaken Him!

The lesson of Rosh Hashanah is that God is alive to us in Jesus! If He were not alive for even one millisecond, all the universe would crumble and cease to exist! "He is before all things, and in him all things hold together" (Colossians 1:17).

Not only is God alive, but also His divine intent is encounter!

During Rosh Hashanah, He creates a vacuum of His presence to stimulate our pursuit of Him. "If you all seek Him, He will be found with you" (2 Chronicles 15:2).

He *wants* us to awaken Him, declare His kingship, and crown Him our sovereign King of kings, Lord of lords, the undisputed Lord of this world and every kingdom of our lives! In ancient times, conquering kings would take the robes of the kings they had defeated and sew them on the end of their robes, forming a long train. The prophet Isaiah's vision of Jesus reflects His absolute Kingship: "In the year that King Uzziah died I saw the Lord sitting on a throne, high and lifted up, and His train filled the temple" (Isaiah 6:1).

To the Jewish mind, crowning God as the sovereign King differs from our Christian understanding, though. Rather than coming as an overpowering force, who "lords" over His people, our blessed Lord Jesus retreats. "I will not force you," He says to His people. "If you crown Me King, it is by your own volition, which I purchased for you on the cross of Calvary." Jesus is never a demanding dictator.

Under the old covenant David said, "Lord, examine me." Under the new covenant, Paul says, "Examine yourself" (1 Corinthians 11:28, NLT).

During Rosh Hashanah and the Days of Awe, which New Testament believers can celebrate every day, may we examine ourselves as we eat the bread and drink the cup of the new covenant. In humility and with a repentant heart, may we seek Him, find Him, and crown Him King. Oh, what a divine encounter awaits us when we do! "As the deer pants for streams of water, so my soul pants for You, O God" (Psalm 42:1, NIV).

Chapter 10

REDEMPTION AT LAST!

But Christ, when He came as a High Priest of the good things to come, by a greater and more perfect tabernacle, not made with hands, that is to say, not of this creation, neither by the blood of goats and calves, but by His own blood, He entered the Most Holy Place once for all, having obtained eternal redemption.

HEBREWS 9:11–12

YOM KIPPUR, OR THE DAY OF ATONEMENT, IS THE HIGHEST and holiest day in the Hebrew calendar. It occurs at the climax of the ten days of repentance—the Days of Awe—and is also the climax of the Season of Teshuvah (te-SHU-vah), the forty-day period commemorating the time Moses spent on the mountain with God, when he received the second set of tablets.

The root word for Kippur is *kafar* (ka-PHAR) which derives from *kofer*. *Kofer* means "ransom" or "redeem." The meaning found in the Psalms translates "to atone by offering a substitute" (Psalm 49:7).

In the Book of Exodus, we find Moses on the mountain with God, lamenting the sins of the Israelites. "Oh, what a great sin these people have committed! They have made themselves gods of gold. But now, please forgive their sin—but if not, then blot me out of the book you have written" (Exodus 32:31–32). Moses is willing to sacrifice his place in God's book if God will spare the people, prefiguring the role of Jesus, whose sacrifice covered all people.

Yom Kippur is the sixth of the major feasts of God and takes place on the tenth day of the seventh month. This is the one day of the year on which the high priest of God was permitted to enter the holy of holies of the temple and make atonement for the sins of God's people. It was a somber day of fasting and humility, as well as deep repentance for the sins of the year.

> The LORD spoke to Moses, saying: Also on the tenth day of this seventh month there shall be the Day of Atonement. It shall be a holy convocation to you, and you shall humble yourselves, and offer a food offering made by fire to the LORD. You shall do no work on that same day, for it is the Day of Atonement to make atonement for you before the LORD your God. For whoever is not humbled on that same day, he shall be cut off from among his people. And whoever does any work in that same day, that person I will destroy from among his people. You shall do no manner of work. It shall be a perpetual statute throughout your generations in all your dwellings. It shall be to you a sabbath of complete rest, and you shall afflict your souls. On the ninth day of the month starting at the evening, from evening to evening, you shall celebrate your sabbath.
> —LEVITICUS 23:26–32

In Leviticus 16:2 God gave detailed instructions as to how Aaron was to enter the holy of holies and make atonement for the people. If you recall, from Leviticus 10, Aaron's sons, Nadab and Abihu, were struck dead by the fire of God when they went about their priestly duties in an unauthorized way. As a result of this incident, God gave specific instructions to Moses.

Tell your brother Aaron that he is not to come whenever he chooses into the Most Holy Place behind the curtain in front of the atonement cover on the ark, or else he will die. For I will appear in the cloud over the atonement cover.

—NIV

The message God was trying to convey to His people was that He is holy and He desires for His people to be holy as well. He wanted them to understand the difference between the holy and the profane, between what He said was clean and unclean.

God is the high King of heaven, and before Jesus came, His people were not to approach Him without invitation and in the prescribed way. This truth hovered over the Day of Atonement. God wanted His people to understand the difference between the profane, ungodly, and occult cultures that surrounded them and His kingdom culture. The Israelites struggled to know the difference and often failed.

As believers operating in the new covenant, we have the freedom to approach God directly, without mediation or sacrifice, because Jesus is our sacrifice. He opened the door so that mediation is no longer necessary. When we contrast life in the new covenant with life under the old covenant we can gain a deeper appreciation for our current status in the kingdom of God.

Consider for a moment the intricate requirements God placed upon the high priest of Israel for entering the holy of holies on the Day of Atonement. The priest was required to wash himself completely before putting on pure linen garments specifically designed to keep all flesh from view.

When he was appropriately attired, he then stood before the Lord, confessing his sins and the sins of his house, as a bull was brought before the Lord. The bull was sacrificed and its blood put into a basin. Then two goats, given by the congregation, were brought before the Lord. Lots were cast and one of these goats was chosen to be the sacrifice and the other to be the "scapegoat."

The high priest then took coals from the brazen altar, put them in a censer, added incense, and proceeded to go behind the veil of the tabernacle, where the smoke of the censer filled the holy of holies.

Next, the high priest would come out of the tabernacle, retrieve the basin of bull's blood, and return to the holy of holies, where he would sprinkle the bull's blood on the ark of the covenant. Once this ritual was complete, he would exit the tabernacle. Outside, he killed the goat chosen for sacrifice and took its blood back into the tabernacle to sprinkle on the ark of the covenant. Then, he would go outside, lay his hands on the remaining goat, confessing the sins of Israel over it, before sending the goat away into an uninhabited land.

This is how God desired to be approached by His people. He wanted purity, with no flesh involved, the shedding of blood, and all sin removed. And He wanted it all done with holy fear and reverence. This was the meaning of the Day of Atonement.

Consider for a moment what it would be like for us if Jesus had not come and died. We would still be a people awaiting access to the presence of God on one day each year; still be hoping for acceptance by the King of the universe based on our deeds. We would still be dependent upon a high priest to make atonement for us with the blood of bulls and goats.

What a sorry state we would be in if Jesus had not come, if He had not become our once and for all High Priest before God. But thanks be to God that Jesus, the Lamb of God, did come for us!

Here are the glorious words from the Book of Hebrews that tell of the finished work of Jesus.

> But Christ, when He came as a High Priest of the good things to come, by a greater and more perfect tabernacle, not made

with hands, that is to say, not of this creation, neither by the blood of goats and calves, but by His own blood, He entered the Most Holy Place once for all, having obtained eternal redemption. For if the blood of bulls and goats, and the ashes of a heifer, sprinkling the unclean, sanctifies so that the flesh is purified, how much more shall the blood of Christ, who through the eternal Spirit offered Himself without blemish to God, cleanse your conscience from dead works to serve the living God?

For this reason He is the Mediator of a new covenant, since a death has occurred for the redemption of the sins that were committed under the first covenant, so that those who are called might receive the promise of eternal inheritance.

—HEBREWS 9:11–15

But this Man, after He had offered one sacrifice for sins forever, sat down at the right hand of God. Since that time He has been waiting for His enemies to be made His footstool. For by one offering He has forever perfected those who are sanctified.

—HEBREWS 10:12–14

Therefore, brothers, we have confidence to enter the Most Holy Place by the blood of Jesus, by a new and living way that He has opened for us through the veil, that is to say, His flesh, and since we have a High Priest over the house of God, let us draw near with a true heart in full assurance of faith, having our hearts sprinkled to cleanse them from an evil conscience, and our bodies washed with pure water.

—HEBREWS 10:19–22

How marvelous! This is now the meaning of the Day of Atonement for God's new covenant people! We no longer need to rely on the blood of bulls and goats or on the purity of a high priest who goes trembling into God's presence once a year. Now, thanks to Jesus our great High Priest, we can "approach the throne of grace with confidence, so that we may receive mercy and find grace to help us in our time of need" (Hebrews 4:16). The Day of Atonement has become an atoned-for life that never ends for God's new covenant people.

THE SEVEN ANOINTINGS
OF THE ATONEMENT

As I mentioned earlier, it's during this fall feast season that our adversary, Satan, wages warfare and unleashes chaos in every imaginable way. Perhaps it is because he knows that the feasts of Passover and Pentecost have been fulfilled, but not the Feast of Tabernacles, which could be the very time Jesus returns for His bride, the church.

From the tragedy of September 11, 2001, to numerous other terror attacks and senseless acts of violence we see on the news every day, the enemy's all-out assaults are all too evident. The stock market plunged in several different years during the time of the fall feasts. Many wars have started during this time, and numerous earthquakes, hurricanes, and volcano eruptions have occurred in the fall of the year.

Perhaps Satan bombards us with such vicious onslaughts during this particular season because he knows the words from the second chapter of Joel:

> Be glad then, ye children of Zion, and rejoice in the LORD your God: for he hath given you the former rain moderately, and he will cause to come down for you the rain, the former rain, and the latter rain in the first month.
>
> —JOEL 2:23, KJV

Did you catch that? You'll receive a double portion from the Lord—the former and the latter rain. We can be sure Satan doesn't want us to get even a single portion, let alone a double portion.

The second chapter of Joel lays out seven anointings of the atonement. These passages can be seen in a new light when we understand the backdrop of the season of tabernacles.

1. The first anointing is the double portion in verse 23.

2. The second anointing is for financial breakthrough: "And the floors shall be full of wheat, and the fats shall overflow with wine and oil." You'll receive a financial breakthrough in your life (Joel 2:24, KJV).

3. The third anointing is the restoration: "And I will restore to you the years that the locust hath eaten, the cankerworm, and the caterpillar, and the palmerworm, my great army which I sent among you" (Joel 2:25, KJV). The devil will be forced to restore the years the locusts have eaten, and nothing you've lost is going to stay lost!

4. The fourth anointing is for provision—special miracles: "And ye shall eat in plenty, and be satisfied, and praise the name of the LORD your God, that hath dealt wondrously with you: and my people shall never be ashamed" (Joel 2:26, KJV).

5. The fifth anointing is the covenant promise: "And ye shall know that I am in the midst of Israel, and that I am the LORD your God, and none else: and my people shall never be ashamed" (Joel 2:26, KJV).

6. The sixth anointing is an increase of revelation knowledge poured into your life and that of your family's lives: "And it shall come to pass afterward, that I will pour out my spirit upon all flesh; and your sons and your daughters shall prophesy, your old men shall dream dreams, your young men shall see visions:" (Joel 2:28, KJV).

7. The seventh anointing is deliverance: "And it shall come to pass, that whosoever shall call on the name of the Lord shall be delivered:" (Joel 2:32, KJV).

Thank God for His abundant blessings in our lives, and the powerful promises in His Word, as we rejoice in the continued revelations of His feast seasons!

Chapter 11

JUBILEE—
GOD'S GRAND DESIGN

Today this Scripture is fulfilled in your hearing.

LUKE 4:21

I MENTIONED THE CONCEPT OF JUBILEE EARLIER, BUT I NEED to deal with it in more detail, because I believe it has an immediate impact on the days in which we are living.

Leviticus chapter 25 relates specific information God relayed to Moses regarding the Sabbath, or Shemitah year, as well as the year of Jubilee. The principle the Lord handed down was an extension of the weekly Sabbath—work six, rest one.

Since God created everything in the universe, it is reasonable to conclude He knows what is best for His creation. This is true for the simplest life forms as well as for the most sophisticated ones. God's plan for the man He created was to spend six days working at what brings him satisfaction and fulfillment, then the divine design was in him to spend one day ceasing from labor and worshipping the One who makes both our work and our worship worthwhile.

God's plan for productivity and rest also extended to the land itself. Jehovah instructed Moses to command the children of

Israel to allow the land He was giving them to rest every seventh year. Afterward they were directed not to sow, reap a harvest from their fields, or gather grapes from their vines. They were permitted to eat whatever they found that grew of itself during the year of rest, but the purpose was to give the land a chance to recuperate from the rigors of producing crops on an annual basis. This was not simply an injunction against putting human effort above trust in God, but it also made good long-term economic sense. As modern farmers have discovered, depleted soil yields less than ground that has been allowed to recover from intensive planting and harvesting cycles. Just as with people who are more productive when properly rested, a year of rest would enable the land to produce more during the "working" years.

At every seventh, or Shemitah year, those Israelites who were sold into servitude as a result of a judgment to pay a debt or because of a crime were set free and debts were forgiven, according to Exodus 21:2 and Deuteronomy 15:1–2, 12.

But that's not all God had in mind. At the end of seven cycles of Sabbath years, Israel was to announce that the fiftieth year was a year of release, or Jubilee. Leviticus 25:10–13 says,

> You shall consecrate the fiftieth year, and proclaim liberty throughout all the land to all the inhabitants. It shall be a Jubilee to you, and each of you shall return to his possession, and every person shall return to his family. That fiftieth year will be a Jubilee for you. You shall neither sow nor reap that which grows by itself, nor gather the grapes of your unpruned vines. For it is the Jubilee. It shall be holy to you. You shall eat the produce of the field. In the Year of Jubilee you shall return to your property.

If anyone had fallen upon difficult times, relief was provided in the year of Jubilee. If someone was forced to sell their property as the result of a disaster or destitution, it was returned at the beginning of the fiftieth year. Homes were restored and hope was kindled in hearts that had hung heavy with dread and drudgery. What had been lost was regained. Those who were far from the promises that God had provided for them received a new beginning. Everyone returned to his rightful possession during this time of release. Jubilee also provided for the freedom of those who had sold themselves into bondage because of poverty. It was a divine "do-over" for everyone in Israel who needed it.

It is certainly not difficult to see how Jubilee is a type of the freedom we have as believers in Jesus Christ. Through the grace of God, we are restored to our rightful inheritance and the chains that bound us are loosed, allowing us to walk into our futures as free people instead of being bound to the sins, habits, and regrets of the past. Jubilee was historically a time of unbridled and unparalleled celebration.

As I write this, the next Jubilee year is rapidly approaching. It begins with the blast of the trumpet announcing the most holy day of the year, the Day of Atonement—which will occur on September 23, 2015. Historically, some of the most catastrophic upheavals in the world have taken place on the eve of Jubilee. We are entering into that period right now. God is arresting our attention, compelling us to be ready to redeem the time. I'm reminded of these words, from Daniel 11:32: "By flatteries he will corrupt those who act wickedly toward the covenant. But the people who know their God will be strong and take action."

This is no time to retreat and seek cover. This is the time, as Isaiah shouted, "Arise, shine, for your light has come, and the glory of the LORD has risen upon you. For the darkness shall cover the earth and deep darkness the peoples; but the LORD shall rise upon you, and His glory shall be seen upon you" (Isaiah 60:1–2). The last act in the drama of human history is about to begin, and God has chosen us to be on the stage for the glorious end. Jubilee is indeed a time of celebration!

Unfortunately it is of interest that there is little evidence recorded in the Bible that Israel observed either the Sabbath or Jubilee years during their time in the Promised Land. Jewish scholars point out that God's condition of counting the Sabbath and Jubilee years was, according to Leviticus 25:2, "When you come into the land that I give you…" All the tribes were required to be situated on their inheritance in order for this time period to begin. Those conditions could have only been fulfilled from the conquest of Canaan until the captivity of the northern kingdom by Assyria and have not existed since then.

Almighty God dramatically warned His people that not allowing the land to enjoy its rest would have disastrous implications. Leviticus 26:33–35 says, "I will scatter you among the nations and I will draw out a sword after you. And your land shall be desolate and your cities a waste. Then the land shall enjoy its sabbaths as long as it lies desolate, while you are in your enemies' land; then the land shall rest and enjoy its sabbaths. As long as it lies desolate it shall rest because it did not rest during your sabbaths when you lived upon it."

This judgment was confirmed in 2 Chronicles 36:20–21:

> Then he carried into exile to Babylon the remnant, who survived the sword, and they were slaves to him and his sons until the kingdom of Persia ruled, to fulfill the word of the Lord by the mouth of Jeremiah, until the land had enjoyed her Sabbaths. As long as she lay desolate, she kept Sabbath, to fulfill seventy years.

It is certainly not my intention to discourage you by this observation of the fulfillment of God's warnings to Israel. Remember with every message of judgment there is also a message of hope for the future. Another of God's messengers is speaking to everyone with ears to hear—this is what the prophet Isaiah said to His people and anyone else with spirits to hear: "And there shall come forth a shoot from the stump of Jesse, and a Branch shall grow out of his roots. The Spirit of the LORD shall rest upon him, the Spirit of wisdom and understanding, the Spirit of counsel and might, the Spirit of knowledge and of the fear of the LORD. He shall delight in the fear of the LORD, he shall not judge by what his eyes see, nor reprove by what his ears hear; but with righteousness he shall judge the poor, and reprove with fairness for the meek of the earth" (Isaiah 11:1–4)

In the Old Testament economy God Almighty revealed many truths that were understood and practiced in the natural, everyday world. While these statutes and laws were good and beneficial in themselves, they had a deeper, more prophetic and profound purpose—to prepare us for an even greater reality that was part of His masterful, magnificent plan for our future.

Jubilee was a time of unrestrained release and restoration for those who had been dispossessed or economically distressed. But Jubilee was much more than just a means by which Jehovah God could allow His people to return to their ancestral allotment of land. It was an opportunity to begin again. The fiftieth year was not a time for looking back to failure, but for looking forward—to a time of fulfillment.

I AM YOUR JUBILEE

During the first century, no Roman official sought a posting in Judea. It was considered a backwater province far from the centers of power and influence in the great Roman Empire. And no

127

part of the place, known to the Romans for its peculiar inhabitants who stubbornly clung to their Jewish religion, was more backward than Galilee.

Even though their temple had been rebuilt, the Jews met in synagogues in their various cities and towns on the Sabbath to worship the living God. The service included readings from the Law and the prophets, prayers, recitation of the Shema, and a commentary or sermon on a portion of Scripture that was read. Any adult Jew who was a part of the synagogue, or even a visitor, was eligible to read. We don't know for sure whether the readings were chosen ahead of time according to a yearly schedule or whether the readers could choose a portion themselves.

It was into a scenario such as this that we see Jesus attending a synagogue that was familiar to Him: "He went to Nazareth, where he had been brought up, and on the Sabbath day he went into the synagogue, as was his custom. And he stood up to read. The scroll of the prophet Isaiah was handed to him. Unrolling it, he found the place where it is written: "The Spirit of the Lord is on me, because he has anointed me to preach good news to the poor. He has sent me to proclaim freedom for the prisoners and recovery of sight for the blind, to release the oppressed, to proclaim the year of the Lord's favor" (Luke 4:16–19, NIV).

It is no coincidence that this passage deals with the fulfillment of the year of Jubilee. Listen to the imagery: good news to the poor, freedom for the prisoners, release for the oppressed, and the year of the Lord's favor—all of these point to the unmistakable characteristics of the fiftieth year. Everyone present understood that Isaiah's announcement dealt with a time when the favor of God would abound and that those who were captive would be set free—regardless of what held them in bondage. However, since Jubilee was a date on a calendar, and not one that had been observed in their current economic circumstances, those present probably didn't see how it applied to them, except in some future age that had little to do with their present situation.

Keep this in mind, as well: Jesus was someone who was well-known to everyone in Nazareth. He had been raised there, as the son of Joseph, part of a large family that had been part of the community for many years. In addition, Jesus had received some recent notoriety for His preaching tour through the synagogues of Galilee. Now He was at home.

But it was what He did next that shocked the congregation. Here is what happened, from Luke 4:20–21: "Then He rolled up the scroll, and He gave it back to the attendant, and sat down. The eyes of all those who were in the synagogue were fixed on Him. And He began to say to them, 'Today this Scripture is fulfilled in your hearing.'"

The indignation among those in attendance that day must have been palpable. In modern vernacular, they questioned, "Who does He think He is?" This may have been because of the words He uttered or because of where He sat down—or both. Debate continues among scholars about whether or not an actual seat was designated as "Moses's seat" where leaders sat in synagogues, or whether the term should be interpreted as teaching from the Law of God. Such actual stone chairs have been unearthed in ruins of synagogues, but whether or not they were designated as Moses's seat we cannot say with certainty. If in fact Jesus sat there, it would have caused great agitation and consternation among those in attendance. In any case, the people became so enraged with Jesus that they attempted to throw Him over a steep cliff, but God supernaturally delivered Him from their wrath.

Here is what He was saying: "Whatever you've been waiting for has just arrived. Jubilee is not a date on a calendar—it's a Person. I am your Jubilee."

Let's take a closer look at Isaiah's words: "The Spirit of the Lord is on me, because He has anointed me…" (v. 18, NIV). The word *anoint* means "to smear" or "to rub." Those who were anointed with oil had oil liberally applied to them, marking them for a particular position of service.

This anointing was not just a little spot of oil—no "little dab will do ya." Anointing took place with entire horns or containers filled with oil. In ancient times, when someone was anointed, there was no mistaking what had happened. Many times the oil included some sort of aromatic fragrance that filled the entire room or vicinity of the person who had received the anointing.

Another way to think of anointing is painting. In Egypt on the evening of the first Passover, the children of Israel were commanded to collect the blood of a lamb, dip a branch of hyssop in it, and then brush it over the doorposts of their homes. Hyssop is a very aromatic shrub that grows in profusion in the Middle East, and using it for the purpose of painting the doorposts would have resulted in an unmistakably bloody and profusely fragrant door.

Our precious Savior was anointed, not sparingly, but in a measure too great to be missed. But it wasn't enough that He was anointed. The anointing was upon His life for the express purpose of fulfilling the will of God, His Father. Again, Isaiah tells us what He was anointed to accomplish.

1. He was anointed to preach, or proclaim, good news to the poor. This included both the poor in spirit as well as the economically disadvantaged. And the best news anyone who has been poor can receive is this: your day of abundance has arrived—spiritually and naturally. The spiritually poor can receive the riches of the gospel, including forgiveness of sins and eternal life. The financially poor can receive the

promise of their needs being met and everything necessary to fulfill God's will for their lives.

2. Jesus came to proclaim freedom to the prisoners. Whatever has held you in bondage is utterly powerless in comparison to the boundless power of the Son of God. The chains that have held you fast must fall because of the anointing of Jesus Christ, who came expressly to destroy every yoke and set every captive free, even as for Paul and Silas, so also for us (Acts 16:26–27). Our chains are broken and the prison doors are open!.

3. Recovery of sight to the blind is another area of divine release that is available as a result of the anointing that our crucified and resurrected King carries. Both physical and spiritual blindness are cured by one touch from the Master's nail-scarred hands (Isaiah 53:5).

4. Release from oppression is another benefit of receiving Jesus's holy anointing. Whatever has kept you back, held you down, or pushed you under must give way to His delivering power. "He delivered us from so great a death and does deliver us. In Him we trust that He will still deliver us" (2 Corinthians 1:10).

5. Jesus announced that He was anointed to proclaim the year of the Lord's favor. The Amplified Bible has this to say about the acceptable year of the Lord: "…the day when salvation and the free favors of God profusely abound." Jubilee is a time when salvation

(deliverance, healing, safety, preservation, and all the blessings of God through Christ by the power of the Holy Ghost) and the free favors of God profusely abound. This in no way is to be interpreted to describe a time that awaits us in the far-distant future. Jesus declared and decreed it so that we could believe and receive it! The time is now!

When the children of Israel painted the doorposts of their houses in obedience to God's command, their actions attracted divine attention. The angel of death who had visited every household in Egypt passed over every home where the blood had been applied. God's favor profusely abounded upon all those who remained under the blood. The icy tentacles of death itself could not touch them. The miracle of God is released by what He does when we simply obey.

In the same fashion, as a result of faith in the blood of Jesus Christ, our Jubilee, the Lord God paints you—marks you, targets you—with a fragrance that verifiably attracts His overwhelming, overflowing blessing and favor. Think about it: God Almighty Himself has placed divine spiritual substance upon you that releases His free favor to seek you out and track you down. You may think the devil has you targeted for destruction, but God surely has you marked for His blessing.

That's not all. Jesus clearly stated that He was anointed by the Spirit of the Lord—but He is not the only one that is eligible to receive this anointing. Listen to these words from Joel 2:28–29:

> And it will be that, afterwards, I will pour out My Spirit on all flesh; then your sons and your daughters will prophesy, your old men will dream dreams, and your young men will see visions. Even on the menservants and maidservants in those days I will pour out My Spirit.

The anointing that you have received from Him remains in you (1 John 2:27)! That means we too are anointed and empowered and called to do the works that Jesus did. The same power that enabled Him to perform the miracles of healing and deliverance that characterized His life and ministry is available to everyone who has accepted Him as Savior and Lord. Your acceptance of this anointing is another fulfillment of the words of the prophet Isaiah that were read by the living Christ in that synagogue in Nazareth so long ago.

But as glorious as that revelation is, it is still not the ultimate fulfillment of the reality of which the year of Jubilee is just a type and shadow. It gets even better—much better—and the better part is nearer than we can imagine.

THE SUFFERING SERVANT

In first-century Judea, messianic fervor was at a fevered pitch. People living in the region chafed under Roman rule and longed for the day when they would be able to govern their own affairs once again. From time to time some self-appointed savior would rise up, convince some people to follow him, and claim to be the one who would follow in the footsteps of the judges of Israel and overthrow the Roman overlords. Inevitably this resistance movement would bow to the might of imperial Rome, and the ringleader would be killed and his followers scattered.

It was into this culture that the Lord Jesus Christ appeared on the scene following His baptism in the Jordan River by John the Baptist, the most powerful prophet Israel had seen since the days of Elijah. Jesus proclaimed the Word of God with power and had an outstanding track record of miracles, signs, and wonders to corroborate His preaching.

People were in such anticipation of a deliverer that on at least one occasion they considered taking Him by force and making

Him a king. But when He spoke to them of trust, obedience, and sacrifice, many of those who followed Him turned back and lost all interest. (See John 6.)

However, as His miraculous ministry continued, His fame continued to spread. Eventually He visited His friends Mary and Martha in Bethany, a short distance from Jerusalem, where His friend Lazarus had died. With one mighty word under that glorious anointing, Jesus raised to life again the four-day-dead body of Lazarus, and death itself bowed its creaking knee. There were two reactions to His action.

The first response was that many people who had been in doubt about exactly who Jesus was got off the fence and believed in Him. The other was that His enemies, the religious leaders, became consolidated in their determination to destroy Him by any means necessary.

As the feast of Passover approached, Jesus returned to Jerusalem in the company of His disciples. Upon entering the holy city, a vast multitude hailed Him, shouting hosannas and hallelujahs, and waving palm branches before Him as He rode triumphantly into town on the colt of a donkey. It must have been an impressive demonstration, because even His enemies exclaimed, "... the world has followed Him" (John 12:19).

But as anyone who has ever spent even the briefest of moments under the glare of the public eye is aware, public opinion is notoriously unpredictable. The very same crowd who hailed His arrival one day was shouting just as loudly for His crucifixion before the week was over.

The key to understanding this is the realization that those who were singing His praises during His arrival fully and completely expected Him to ride into town as a conquering king, dispossess the trespassing and overbearing Romans, set up an earthly kingdom, and lead them all into a victorious and prosperous future. They failed to recognize that all the prophecies about a coming King were prefaced by just as many prophetic pronouncements about a suffering Servant.

So when Jesus did not capitalize on what amounted to a political demonstration and was eventually arrested, tried, and condemned to death, the disappointment of the masses knew no bounds. As our suffering, silent Lamb of God stood before the Roman governor Pontius Pilate, it was relatively easy for the religious elite to persuade the furious mod to demand His crucifixion. According to their self-centered, myopic view, Jesus was not the Messiah they expected. In their minds He was just the latest in a long line of imposters who failed to deliver the freedom they craved—the Messiah du jour—and the cruel death of the cross was exactly what He deserved for His deception and ruse.

Listen to this exchange between the Roman governor and the Jewish King recorded in John 18:33–37:

> Again Pilate entered the Praetorium, called Jesus, and said to Him, "Are You the King of the Jews?"
>
> Jesus answered him, "Are you speaking of your own accord, or did others tell you about Me?"
>
> Pilate answered, "Am I a Jew? Your own nation and the chief priests handed You over to me. What have You done?"
>
> Jesus answered, "My kingdom is not of this world. If My kingdom were of this world, then My servants would fight, that I would not be handed over to the Jews. But now My kingdom is not from here."
>
> Therefore Pilate said to Him, "Then are You a king?"
>
> Jesus answered, "You say correctly that I am a king. For this reason I was born, and for this reason I came into the world, to bear witness to the truth. Everyone who is of the truth hears My voice."

Do you see it? Jesus said, "My kingdom is not of this world." But, mark these words well, there is coming a day when it will be! In His first advent, He came as a baby in a manger, a servant riding on a donkey, and a bleeding sacrificial Lamb nailed to the angry, mean, and biting beam called Calvary. But the next time He appears, His glory and majesty will be unmistakable. He will return as the King of kings and Lord of lords. And, according to Revelation 20:6, He will lead His people to an unimaginably glorious thousand-year reign on Earth, of which the prophets also foretold.

What does this have to do with the year of Jubilee? From the very first words of your Bible, a fundamental principle is expressed: everything in the natural world is divinely connected to the spirit realm. Even though we can't see it with our eyes or feel it with our fingers, the spiritual realm is more real than the pages you are reading right now. All that we can see came from a place we cannot see.

Jubilee had to first be manifested in the spirit before it could ever be demonstrated as a spiritual reality. First was the type of the freedom that was available in a year of release and restoration. Then came Jesus Christ, the anointed One, who offered true freedom to everyone who would trust in Him as Savior and Lord—the spiritual fulfillment of the shadow seen in the Old Testament fiftieth year. But finally, we who believe in Him will experience the complete and total fulfillment of Jubilee, as we rule and reign with Him for a thousand years. Only God knows what we will experience after that as we receive His loving kindness for the endless ages of eternity.

Chapter 12

DWELLING WITH GOD

I will set My tabernacle among you, and I shall
not abhor you. I will walk among you, and I will
be your God, and you shall be My people.

LEVITICUS 26:11–12

THE SEASON OF TABERNACLES CAN BE DIVIDED INTO TWO
distinct portions. The first portion consists of the period
of time comprising Rosh Hashanah, Yom Kippur, and the Days
of Awe, and is a time of examination. The second portion is the
Feast of Tabernacles, a time of celebration and intimacy.

The Feast of Tabernacles is the seventh and final fall festival
of God, occurring on the fifteenth day of the seventh month,
which would always be the seventh full moon of the year. It
concludes the fall season of festival feasts and is also the final
pilgrimage feast.

Sukkot (soo-KOTE) is the Hebrew name for this feast, which
means "booths." More than anything else, this feast is about the
people of God recalling God's provision of shelter (booths) in the
desert when they first came out of Egypt. It is a great occasion of
remembrance and of gratitude.

> The LORD said to Moses, "Say to the Israelites: 'On the fifteenth day of the seventh month the LORD's Festival of Tabernacles begins, and it lasts for seven days....On the first day you are to take branches from luxuriant trees—from palms, willows and other leafy trees—and rejoice before the LORD your God for seven days.
>
> "'Celebrate this as a festival to the Lord...each year....Live in temporary shelters for seven days: All native-born Israelites are to live in such shelters so your descendants will know that I had the Israelites live in temporary shelters when I brought them out of Egypt. I am the LORD your God.'"
>
> —LEVITICUS 23:33–43, NIV

On Sukkot, observant Jews build temporary shelters, called "sukkahs" or booths, on rooftops in, backyards, and even on balconies. These structures symbolize dependence on God. According to Jewish tradition, each booth can reach only twenty cubits in height; however, there is no limit to their length or width. Sukkahs must have at least three sides and be large enough for an entire family, as well as guests, because the Feast of Tabernacles symbolizes unity and is all about inviting others to celebrate the goodness of God.

We know from studying Jewish tradition that tabernacles, or Sukkot, corresponds with the time of the fruit harvest for the early Jews. The fruit harvest occurred at the end of fall harvest season, when the fruit of all the season's crops was counted, and the people rejoiced in the abundance of God's provision. It was a joyous time.

For the church today, Sukkot is still a joyous time of celebration, representing our new covenant access to God, thanks to the work of our great High Priest, Jesus Christ. Now we are all members of His body, the church, and as such, we celebrate together His great Feast of Tabernacles, remembering His great love and provision for us. Jesus did come to tabernacle with us, so that we might be redeemed, cleansed from sin, and now eagerly await His final return in glory when He will tabernacle with us once again for all eternity!

THE LULAV (LOO-lahv)

The festival of Sukkot has three main symbols. There is the booth (the *sukkah)*, the *lulav*, and the *etrog.* The *lulav* is a palm branch, tied together with two willow branches and three myrtle branches. It is of interest to note that "myrtle," or "Hadassah" was Esther's Hebrew name, Esther 2:7:

> And he brought up Hadassah, that is, Esther, his uncle's daughter: for she had neither father nor mother, and the maid was fair and beautiful; whom Mordecai, when her father and mother were dead, took for his own daughter.

The *etrog* is a lemon-like fruit. It looks like a lumpy lemon but smells heavenly. During each day of Sukkot, except the Shabbat, the *lulav* and *etrog* are ceremoniously waved. The instructions for all of this are found in Leviticus 23:40:

> And ye shall take you on the first day the boughs of goodly trees, branches of palm trees, and the boughs of thick trees, and willows of the brook; and ye shall rejoice before the Lord your God seven days.
>
> —KJV

Each day the people are to wave the *lulav* and the *etrog* in six directions—north, south, east, west, above, and below—declaring that God is surrounding and encompassing them in every direction. How comforting to know that our praises lift up a shield of favor for us in every direction. "For surely, O Lord, you bless the righteous; you surround them with your favor as with a shield" (Psalm 5:12, NIV).

The coming together of the *lulav* and the *etrog* in praise is symbolic of a body in harmony, with all parts functioning in their respective places. As New Testament believers, this symbolism draws us to the revelation of the body (the church) given to us by the Apostle Paul in 1 Corinthians: "The body is a unit, though it is made up of many parts; and though all its parts are many, they form one body. So it is with Christ. For we were all baptized by one Spirit into one body—whether Jew or Greeks, slave or free—and we were all given the one Spirit to drink" (1 Corinthians 12:12–13, NIV).

As we examine the *lulav* more closely, we see a metaphor: the spine of the body is represented by the long straight palm branch, the eye by the small oval myrtle leaf, the mouth by the long oval willow leaf, and the heart by the *etrog* fruit. Each of these parts of the body can be used for sinful indulgences, but God directs us to use them as members of righteousness.

> Neither yield ye your members as instruments of unrighteousness unto sin: but yield yourselves unto God, as those that are alive from the dead, and your members as instruments of righteousness unto God.
>
> —ROMANS 6:13, KJV

Another interpretation of the *lulav* is that it is symbolic of the different kinds of people that make up the Jewish people. New Testament believers can easily see them as the church.

The *etrog* is seen as having both a taste and an aroma, just like the people of Israel who have both Torah learning and good deeds. For New Testament believers, the church includes those who possess a knowledge of God's Word and are also "doers" of the Word.

The fruit of the *lulav* has taste but no aroma, symbolizing the people of Israel who have Torah but no good deeds. For New Testament believers, the church includes those who possess a knowledge of God's Word but are not "doers" of the Word.

The myrtle has an aroma but not a taste, like the people of Israel who have good deeds but do not have Torah. For New Testament believers, the church includes those who are doers of God's Word but do not possess a knowledge of the Word.

Then there is the willow, which has no taste and no aroma, symbolizing the people of Israel who do not have Torah and do not have good deeds. God says, "Let them all bond together in one bundle and atone for each other." Hence, the waving of the *lulav* and the *etrog* at Sukkot.

For New Testament believers, the symbolism of the willow includes those who possess neither a knowledge of God's Word nor are they "doers" of His Word. In other words, they are those who have not yet accepted Christ as Lord and Savior. But we must remember they are yet the creation of God, and I believe He will yet have them, for He desires that not one should perish (2 Peter 3:9).

We gain tremendous insight into the nature of our God through His prescriptions for His feasts. He wants His people to celebrate their love for Him with dancing, singing, shouting, and declarations, often using the very blessings that He has graciously provided. It is for this very reason that He loves a wave offering of sheaves of grain during the Feast of Firstfruits, and why He desires loaves to be waved on Pentecost and the branches of vibrant trees of the land He has granted to His people to be waved before Him and held aloft in gratitude at Tabernacles. In His great love for us, He has provided so beautifully for our every need, and He invites us to join in rejoicing with Him in this overflow of His love.

You see, the Feast of Tabernacles is not merely a religious regulation. God did not institute this feast because He needed to be reminded of what He had done. He has designed these feasts to define the relationship He will have with His people. They are a call to a divine encounter with God.

Sukkot also means "dwelling place" and "secret place," where the Almighty covers us with His wings, overshadows us with His presence, and leaves us filled with His glory and power, and with the expectation of purposes yet untold. Sukkot is dwelling as one with the living God.

Jesus celebrated Tabernacles when He walked the earth. We see this in the Book of John chapter 7. Jesus had gone to Jerusalem, to the Feast of Tabernacles, in secret, because there were those who were looking to kill Him. But halfway through the festival, He began to teach. His words stirred the hearts of many. Some were amazed, while others grew angry. Opposition broke out, and there was such a stir that the chief priests and Pharisees sent men to arrest Jesus, but they could not lay a hand on Him.

> On the last and greatest day of the feast, Jesus stood and cried out, "If anyone is thirsty, let him come to Me and drink. He who believes in Me, as the Scripture has said, out of his heart shall flow rivers of living water."
>
> —JOHN 7:37–38

During the Feast of Tabernacles, on the seventh day of the feast, a special day called Hoshana Rabbah (hoe-SHAH-nah rah-BAH) or "the Great Salvation," the high priest would fill a golden pitcher with water, return to the courtyard of the temple, and pour the water out on the altar. Keep this ceremony in mind as you picture Jesus on this same day, shouting at the top of His voice in the same courtyard, "Let anyone who is thirsty come to me and drink. Whoever believes in me, as Scripture has said, rivers of living water will flow from within them."

Jesus was fearless, wasn't He? The high priest might have his golden pitcher filled with water from a local pool, but the living Christ declared before all men and for all time that He offered something far greater. To those who believed, He would give rivers of living water and they would never cease. The high priest's pitcher would quickly run out of water, but Jesus never runs out of His living water. This is something to celebrate!

It is said that at the feast of Sukkot judgment is made concerning the waters, which means that the amount of rain over the next few months, after Rosh Hashanah, would impact the next harvest. But our mighty King of glory says, "Therefore with joy shall ye draw water out of the wells of salvation" (Isaiah 12:3, KJV). How "blessed are they which do hunger and thirst after righteousness: for they shall be filled" (Matthew 5:6, KJV).

This theme of living water resounds throughout the Gospels. One of the most prominent is the encounter Jesus had with the Samaritan woman at the well.

> Jesus said to her, "Everyone who drinks of this water will thirst again, but whoever drinks of the water that I shall give him will never thirst. Indeed, the water that I shall give him will become in him a well of water springing up into eternal life."
>
> —JOHN 4:13–14

Do you see that Tabernacles is a call to relationship, a call to power; to infilling with the Spirit of the living God? It is a call to us, to dwell with the Holy One of Israel. Is it any wonder that Paul yearned for this cohabitation with God, and felt incomplete without it?

> For in this we groan, earnestly desiring to be clothed with
> our habitation which is from heaven.
>
> —2 CORINTHIANS 5:2, NIV

Now that you understand Sukkot, you can see that Paul is referring to it when he uses the word *habitation*. He is declared that no dwelling on this earth will satisfy us once we have experienced life in the sukkot of God. So we groan. Oh, how we groan, with yearning, until our dwelling from heaven is restored.

USHPIZIN—
WELCOMING OUR GUESTS

> Be joyful at your feast—you, your sons and daughters, your
> menservants and maidservants, and the Levites, the aliens,
> the fatherless and the widows who live in your towns.
>
> —DEUTERONOMY 16:14, NIV

From this verse in Deuteronomy and many other places in the Bible, we are taught that when we eat and drink, we should also feed strangers, orphans, and widows, because true joy is shared joy. Jewish custom celebrates this shared joy with the ritual of *ushpizin* (ush-peh-ZIN), which means "welcoming guests."

This ritual occurs during Sukkot. According to Jewish tradition, on each of the seven nights of Sukkot, one of the holy men of Israel is symbolically invited to join the household celebration in the family sukkah, or booth. Ushpizin is actually the prayer of invitation that is recited each night.

As each guest visits the sukkah, he empowers those gathered there with his particular anointing and enlightens with his unique revelation of our Father God. Let's take a look together at these supernatural guests, and what they mean for the church today.

First there is Abraham of the old covenant, who embodies loving-kindness as found in Genesis 13:8–9: "And Abram said unto Lot, Let there be no strife, I pray thee, between me and thee, and between my herdmen and thy herdmen; for we be brethren. Is not the whole land before thee? Separate thyself, I pray thee, from me: if thou wilt take the left hand, then I will go to the right; or if thou depart to the right hand, then I will go to the left" (KJV).

Jesus demonstrated loving-kindness in Mark 10:13–14, "And they brought young children to him, that he should touch them: and his disciples rebuked those that brought them. But when Jesus saw it, he was much displeased, and said unto them, "Suffer the little children to come unto me, and forbid them not: for of such is the kingdom of God."

Next, we have Isaac who portrays strength. Genesis 26:19–22 says,

> But when Isaac's servants dug in the valley and found a well of running water there, the herdsmen of Gerar contended with Isaac's herdsmen, saying, "The water is ours." So he called the name of the well Esek, because they contended with him. They dug another well and quarreled over that also. So he called the name of it Sitnah. Then he moved away from there and dug another well, and they did not quarrel over it. So he called the name of it Rehoboth, for he said, "For now the LORD has made room for us, and we will be fruitful in the land."

Jesus portrayed strength in John 18:4–6, at the time of His arrest:

> Jesus therefore, knowing everything that would happen to Him, went forward and said to them, "Whom do you seek?" They answered Him, "Jesus of Nazareth." Jesus said to them, "I am He." And Judas, who betrayed Him, was standing with them. When He said, "I am He," they drew back and fell to the ground.

The soldiers had come to arrest a meek Jewish peasant and instead encountered the power of God in the flesh.

The third supernatural guest is Jacob, who represents truth.

> So Jacob was left alone, and a man wrestled with him till daybreak. When the man saw that he could not overpower him, he touched the socket of Jacob's hip so that his hip was wrenched as he wrestled with the man. Then the man said, "Let me go, for it is daybreak." But Jacob replied, "I will not let you go unless you bless me." The man asked him, "What is your name?" "Jacob," he answered. Then the man said, "Your name will no longer be Jacob, but Israel, because you have struggled with God and with men and have overcome.
>
> —GENESIS 32:24–28, NIV

Jesus is the truth according to John 14:6: "I am the way, the truth, and the life. No one comes to the Father except through Me."

Next, we have Moses, who personifies the eternal word. "When [the Lord] had made an end of communing with him on Mount Sinai, He gave Moses the two tablets of testimony, tablets of stone, written with the finger of God" (Exodus 31:18).

Jesus is the living Word, according to John 1:1: "In the beginning was the Word, and the Word was with God, and the Word was God."

Aaron is the fifth supernatural guest. He exemplifies divine splendor and majesty. "The LORD said to Moses: Speak to Aaron your brother so that he does not come at any time into the Holy Place within the veil before the mercy seat, which is on the ark, so that he will not die, for I will appear in the cloud on the mercy seat" (Leviticus 16:2).

Jesus exemplifies divine splendor and majesty in Matthew 17:1–2, "After six days Jesus took Peter, James, and John his brother and brought them up to a high mountain alone, and was transfigured before them. His face shone as the sun, and His garments became white as the light." John 17:5, "And now, O Father, glorify Me in Your own presence with the glory which I had with You before the world existed."

The sixth supernatural guest is Joseph. He exhibits spiritual foundation and holiness. "Now Joseph was handsome and well-built. After a time, his master's wife took notice of Joseph and said, 'Lie with me.' But he refused and said to his master's wife, 'My master does not concern himself with anything concerning me in the house, and he has committed all that he has to my charge. There is none greater in this house than I. He has kept nothing back from me but you, because you are his wife. How then can I do this great wickedness and sin against God?' She spoke to Joseph every day, but he did not listen to her about lying with her or being with her" (Genesis 39:6–10).

Jesus exhibits spiritual foundation and holiness to us in Hebrews 4:15, "For we do not have a High Priest who cannot sympathize with our weaknesses, but One who was in every sense tempted like we are, yet without sin."

The seventh and last supernatural guest to be invited to Sukkot is David, who symbolizes the establishment of the kingdom and sovereignty as found in 2 Samuel 7:11–13, 16. "...I will give you rest from all of your enemies. The LORD declares to you that He will instead bring about a house for you. When your days are complete and you lie down with your fathers, I will raise up after you an offspring from your body, and I will establish his rule. He will build a house for My name, and I will establish his royal throne forever.... Your house and dominion will endure before Me forever, and your throne will be established by the LORD forever."

God the Father has given us King Jesus and has established His kingdom and His sovereign rule over all of creation. "But the angel said to her, 'Do not be afraid, Mary, for you have found favor with God. Listen, you will conceive in your womb and bear a Son and shall call His name Jesus. He will be great, and will be called the Son of the Highest. And the Lord God will give Him the throne of His father David, and He will reign over the house of Jacob forever. And of His kingdom there will be no end'" (Luke 1:30–33).

The pattern of ushpizin provides us with a wonderful opportunity for evangelism. Invite those you know and love and the poor and the stranger to your home to share the good news of the Gospel of Jesus Christ with them. Don't wait! The harvest is plentiful!

I invite you to embrace all of God's Word, from both covenants every day with the expectation to experience a divine encounter! God is waiting for you, and His living Word is one of the best places to meet with Him.

A TIME OF INGATHERING

The season of Tabernacles is a time of remembrance, gratitude, and joy, but it is also a time of ingathering. In fact, another Hebrew name for the Feast of Tabernacles is *Chag Ha-asif* or "the Feast of Ingathering."

In the agriculture of Israel, Passover related to the planting season, Pentecost related to the grain harvest, and Sukkot, or Tabernacles, was identified with the fruit harvest.

This may explain the theme of joy in the season of Tabernacles more fully. Crops planted in spring don't bring their full "joy" until they reach their full maturity in the fall. Thus, the harvesters' true rejoicing won't come until the fall, when all crops are harvested and the supplies are stored for the following year. It is then, when the storehouses are full and the fullness of rejoicing begins.

We know that the Feast of Tabernacles is a time of remembrance, but it also has prophetic meaning. The seven days of living in booths envisions *olam haba* (OH-lahm HAH-bah), the world to come, and the millennial reign of Jesus on Earth, when our Lord will "tabernacle" with us during His reign from Zion. This explains much of the theme of joy associated with this feast. When God is near, dwelling with us, protecting us, and providing for us in this world, there is joy!

I believe this is why the Feast of Tabernacles is the only feast in the Bible commanded for all nations. To celebrate this feast is to affirm God's provident care and merciful governance of the world. The Bible says that all nations will have to come to this in time or they will find themselves outside the blessing of God.

Listen to these powerful words:

> Then it will be that all the nations who have come against Jerusalem and survived will go up each year to worship the King, the Lord of Hosts, and to celebrate the Feast of Tabernacles. And it will happen that if any of the families of the earth do not go up to Jerusalem to worship the King, the Lord of Hosts, then there will not be rain for them.
>
> If the family of Egypt does not go up and enter in, they shall have no rain. This will be the plague with which the Lord strikes the nations that do not go up to celebrate the Feast of Tabernacles. This will be the punishment of Egypt and the punishment of all the nations who do not go up to celebrate the Feast of Tabernacles.
>
> —ZECHARIAH 14:16–19

There is power in the Feast of Tabernacles and in God's feasts in general. They are conduits of His blessings and part of the way we acknowledge Him. The celebration of these feasts and what they embody are necessary for all the nations of the world, not just individuals or churches. Ultimately all nations will observe the feasts of God in Jerusalem or they will be excluded from the blessing and protection of God. This moves the feasts from merely matters of historical memory and religious duty, to the heart of what it means to submit to God's authority and rule. There is no mistaking: God is calling all nations to affirm that He is King of the universe and that He is our Provider!

SHEMINI ATZERET

There is a beautiful and fascinating final feature of the Feast of Tabernacles we have not yet examined. You remember that this feast is seven days long, yet God required an additional eighth day, as stipulated in Numbers 29:35, "On the eighth day you will have a solemn assembly. You will do no ordinary work on it."

This eighth day is called *Shemini Atzeret* (SHMEE-nee aht-ZEH-reht). *Atzeret* means to "abide, tarry or hold back." The wise rabbis through the centuries have concluded that it is as though God is asking those who have observed Sukkot to stay another day and "tarry" with Him, to remain with Him just a little while longer. It reminds us how much God loves our companionship.

I am always so moved by one of the ancient teachings on Shemini Atzeret that says, "You may compare it to a king who had a festival for seven days and invited all the nations of the world to the seven days of feasting. When the seven days were over and the guests had gone, he said to his friend (Israel), 'Let us now have a small meal together, just you and I.'"[1]

This is so beautiful, so transforming! The God of the universe calls us to His dwelling place, where He stirs us to worship Him in the intimacy of His blessing and presence and then says, in essence, "Stay a while longer. I love you. I would have you near another day." My heart leaps at the very thought of this. Is it any wonder that Tabernacles is the final feast of the seven major feasts of God?

Through the years, teachers and mystics have viewed this festival as a sign of eternity. We will dwell with our God, and He, in turn, will dwell with us, even bidding us to tarry with Him forever in an eternity of celebration and fellowship, where we will tabernacle with Him and He with us forever!

> This is the covenant that I will make with the house of Israel after those days, says the Lord: I will put My laws into their minds and write them on their hearts; and I will be their God, and they shall be My people.
> —HEBREWS 8:10

The Apostle John shouts this covenant promise from the island of Patmos in Revelation 21:3:

> And I heard a loud voice from heaven, saying, "Look! The tabernacle of God is with men, and He will dwell with them. They shall be His people, and God Himself will be with them and be their God.

Oh, let us "consider how much love the Father has given to us, that we should be called children of God" (1 John 3:1).

An interesting event occurred on Shemini Atzeret concerning the Lord Jesus Christ. John 8 tells us that Jesus returned to the temple on this day and declared in John 8:12, "I am the light of the world. Whoever follows Me shall not walk in the darkness, but shall have the light of life." And it was shortly thereafter in John 9:5–11 that Jesus healed a man blind from birth, thereby miraculously enabling him to see "the light of the world"!

SIMCHAT TORAH—
THE WORD OF GOD IS NEVER ENDING

Jesus says to us in Matthew 24:35, "Heaven and earth will pass away, but My words will never pass away." In Israel there is another celebration on Tishrei 22 called *Simchat Torah*. Simchat Torah is defined as "rejoicing in the Torah" and marks the completion of the annual cycle of Torah reading, which then begins again immediately.

This unending cycle symbolizes the never-ending and inexhaustible Word of God. Let us remember the words of King Solomon: "My son, attend to my words; incline your ear to my sayings. Do not let them depart from your eyes; keep them in the midst of your heart; for they are life to those who find them, and health to all their body" (Proverbs 4:20).

Chapter 13

THE EMBRACE OF GOD

Embracing what God does for you is the best thing you
can do for him. Don't become so well-adjusted to your cul-
ture that you fit into it without even thinking. Instead, fix
your attention on God. You'll be changed from the inside
out. Readily recognize what he wants from you, and quickly
respond to it. Unlike the culture around you, always drag-
ging you down to its level of immaturity, God brings the
best out of you, develops well-formed maturity in you.

ROMANS 12:1–2, THE MESSAGE

MY LOVELY WIFE, JONI, IS THE PERFECT BALANCE TO MY personality. She is rarely emotional or outwardly expressive—or loud. However, on one occasion she changed my paradigm by weeping. It wasn't necessarily the tears that changed my revelation of God and my relationship with Him but rather where those tears were falling. They were not dripping from her precious chin onto an altar. We weren't in our prayer meeting or receiving holy communion. We weren't even in church or in the presence of others. In fact, she didn't even know I was observing her. But I was there in the room with her, as her tears flowed from her eyes and splashed into dishwater in our kitchen sink.

When I made my presence known by asking her why she wept,

she simply said, "I just realized that as I fulfill my calling as a wife and mother, God receives it as worship. He has visited me here in the everydayness of my life, and I am overwhelmed by His love and presence."

What Joni was experiencing that day at the kitchen sink is summed up by the Apostle Paul in the Book of Romans. This translation from The Message Bible says it clearly:

> So here's what I want you to do, God helping you: Take your everyday, ordinary life—your sleeping, eating, going-to-work, and walking-around life—and place it before God as an offering. Embracing what God does for you is the best thing you can do for him. Don't become so well-adjusted to your culture that you fit into it without even thinking. Instead, fix your attention on God. You'll be changed from the inside out.
>
> —ROMANS 12:1–2

Notice what God said here: "So here's what I want [not command] you to do." We need His help in life, which He will always graciously provide, however, we must understand that the responsibility is ours.

Furthermore, what is to be offered in this instance is our body, not our spirit. I believe God is saying in this passage that He desires "all of us." We are to take our bodies, or our earthliness ("your sleeping, eating, going-to-work, and walking-around life"), and place it all before God as an "offering" or, as the King James Version says, "a living sacrifice." This same deep and glorious revelation is found in Sukkot.

There has been a divorce in the church, where we separate the perceived spiritual aspects of our relationship with the living Christ from the perceived natural aspects of that relationship. Our Father desires for us to thrive in this earth not simply to survive in it. "Living" to me denotes vibrancy, vitality, energy, and motion! I often say that I want to live out loud!

Through the revelation of Sukkot, God says that He wants to become involved in our "everydayness." He wants to be with us when we brush our teeth, drive the kids to school, sit through a sales meeting, write that term paper, make the bed, wash the dishes, mow the lawn, or go to dinner with friends—everything.

Think of it this way: God wants to move in with you. He doesn't desire temporary living arrangements. He doesn't want visitation rights; He wants habitation rights. Sukkot declares He wants a permanent home with us! When you think about it, that's what the elegant Garden of Eden was all about—God establishing a home and people to share it with.

Home is a place of comfort and consolation, a place of relaxation and repose, where you (and God) can just be yourself—your real self. No pretenses, no masks, no filters. Just the joy of being with those who know you and accept you and love you as you are. Home is shelter, which is the most basic of necessities. "For You have been a refuge for me, and a strong tower from the enemy" (Psalm 61:3). What a thought—to be at home in the everydayness of our earthly journey with our God.

Recently I had the opportunity to go back home, not to the place of my birth nor of my present residence, but rather to the place of my ancestry. Home for me is Appalachia, the streams and hollows, the deep dark hills of eastern Kentucky.

Whether it's the mountains ablaze with autumn's majesty or a humble home perched on a hillside, these are the sights of home for me. The fragrance of a freshly mown field or fatback frying in a black iron skillet—these are the smells of home. And the harmony of a gospel quartet or a coal truck in low gear laboring up the mountainside—these are the sounds of home.

Popular culture has capitalized on this instinctive impulse, this divine drive we have to get back home. Do you remember Dorothy and her little dog, Toto, in *The Wizard of Oz*? They were transported by a tornado to a land beyond time, the magical land of Oz, where they witnessed wonders, passed through perils, and encountered companions who propelled them toward their primary purpose. But through it all, Dorothy just wanted to get back home.

At the end of the movie when Dorothy woke up, her wish had come true. She was back home with her family and friends in the familiar surroundings that meant so much to her. It was then that she uttered these words that are indelibly etched on the consciousness of a generation: "There's no place like home."

Truer words have never been spoken, because whether it's a plush penthouse, a tattered tent, a millionaire's mansion, or a country cabin, "there's no place like home."

Home is where your family welcomes you, your friends remember you, there is provision for your needs, protection from attack, your hurts are healed, and you can feel like you're somebody even when you know you ain't nobody. Home is where the heart is.

The Lord Jesus drew reference to God the Father's desired permanent living arrangements with us in John 17:21, "that they may all be one, as You, Father, are in Me, and I in You."

Solomon described the divine encounter beautifully in Song of Songs 2:6, "His left hand is under my head, and his right arm embraces me." The parallel drawn is this: the left hand represents judgment, keeping at a distance, while the right hand illustrates love, acceptance, and being drawn to God.

Rosh Hashanah, Yom Kippur, and Days of Awe demonstrate the left hand of God placed upon our head, which symbolizes the highest part of our encounter—that relationship between God and our human spirit. With His right arm, He embraces us, placing His arm around our back as if to say, "I want all of your life, even your back, which cannot reciprocate My love or devotion." The love of God reaches even to the "back part" of our lives, even to the most insignificant and mundane moments of our earthly existence. "I refuse to let any part of your life go," He says.

God wants all of us. He wants to squeeze close to us, in a breathtaking embrace, even in those ordinary times, when what we are doing seems to have nothing to do with spirituality. "I'll [God] meet you where you live, and I'll love you as you are, not as you should be...because you're never going to be as you should be."[1] This is the unfailing and unfaltering love of our Father expressed through His gift—the supreme sacrifice of His only begotten Son.

Jesus, nailed by tempered spikes through tortured skin into splintered wood, with welcoming arms outstretched announces, "Do I love you? Yes! Yes! A billion times, yes! I love you yesterday, today, and forever. I love you through every storm and tempest, every struggle and temptation, from heaven to earth, to hell, back to earth, and to heaven again. I love you in life and living, in death and dying. I love you. How much? Stretch out your arms. That much and more. I will not leave you here without Me, nor will I remain in heaven without you. I will bring us together again, and we will never be separated, for I am your Father and you are forever My child!"

Mankind once enjoyed an intimate relationship of divine encounter in the Garden of Eden (Genesis 2). By their sin, our pristine parents Adam and Eve estranged themselves and thereby the entire human race from this relationship. Ever since that moment, when sin entered the bloodstream of humanity and a chasm was created between Creator and creation, God sought a way to once again live at home in the midst of His people.

The temporary dwellings Israel built during Tabernacles were reminiscent of a time when God Himself dwelt in the midst of Israel as they made their way through the wilderness. In Exodus 33:14 God told Moses, "My Presence will go with you, and I will give you rest."

We know that God's presence remained in the tabernacle during their wilderness wanderings, according to Exodus 40:34–38:

> Then the cloud covered the tent of meeting, and the glory of the LORD filled the tabernacle. Moses was not able to enter into the tent of meeting because the cloud settled on it, and the glory of the LORD filled the tabernacle. When the cloud was lifted up from over the tabernacle, the children of Israel would set out in all their journeys. But if the cloud was not lifted up, then they did not set out until the day that it was lifted. For the cloud of the LORD was on the tabernacle by day, and fire was on it by night, in the sight of all the house of Israel, throughout all their journeys.

After Israel came into the Promised Land and the temple was built, God's presence remained there, according to 2 Chronicles 5:13–14:

> When the trumpet players and singers made one sound to praise and give thanks to the LORD, and when they lifted up their voice with the trumpets and cymbals and all the instruments of music and praised the LORD saying, "For He is good and His mercy endures forever," that the house, the house of the LORD, was filled with a cloud. And the priests were not able to stand in order to serve because of the cloud, for the glory of the LORD had filled the house of God.

As New Testament believers, we have the presence of God with us and in us: "'And remember, I am with you always, even to the end of the age.' Amen." (Matthew 28:20); "for He has said: 'I will never leave you, nor forsake you'" (Hebrews 13:5, KJV).

This is taken from two Old Testament scriptures:

> Then David said to Solomon his son, "Be strong and coura-geous, and take action. Do not be afraid nor be dismayed for the LORD God, my God, is with you. He will not leave you nor forsake you..."
>
> —1 CHRONICLES 28:20

> As I was with Moses, I will be with you. I will not abandon you. I will not leave you.
>
> —JOSHUA 1:5

As believers, we can celebrate the promise of Tabernacles every day, since God is personally present with us as Jehovah Shammah. Wherever He is becomes our "there." Psalm 133:3 says:

> As the dew of Hermon, that descends upon the mountains of Zion, for there the LORD has commanded the blessing, even life forever.

Chapter 14

DELIVERANCE AND VICTORY

*Now we look inside, and what we see is that anyone
united with the Messiah gets a fresh start, is created
new. The old life is gone; a new life burgeons [prospers]!*

2 CORINTHIANS 5:17, THE MESSAGE

COME WITH ME NOW TO A FEAST THAT IS NOT PART OF THE
original seven feasts of God, and I will show you how we
should make the *mo'edim* (the appointed times of God) not a
matter of history alone, but a matter of experience in Jesus our Lord.

The Feast of Purim takes place in the month of Adar, which is
unique among all the months in the Hebrew calendar. Since the
Hebrew calendar is a lunar calendar, the months are 29.5 days
long, because that's how long it takes to progress from a sliver-
like crescent moon to a dark moon. Our Jewish friends celebrate
the feast of Purim, and although you won't find it commanded by
God in your Bible, you will find the story that gave rise to it in
the Book of Esther. I invite you to walk with me now through the
story of Purim, so that you too can know its power and experience its blessings in your life.

In our solar calendar, one year in every four is longer than the
others, so some time has to be made up every year. The way we do
this is by designating a "leap year." In the Hebrew calendar, this

discrepancy in time is dealt with in the month of Adar. Every so often, when it is needed, a year in the Hebrew calendar is called *shanah meuberet* (shah-NAH mee-oo-BEH-ret), which means "pregnant year." It is so named because this year is pregnant with an extra month. In this pregnant year, the month of Adar happens twice: Adar I and Adar II. This extra month is "born" every so often, when needed.

Purim takes place in a pregnant month, and that fact alone grants us revelation. We are instantly reminded that Jesus came in the "fullness of the time," according to Galatians 4:4—He came when the time was "pregnant." Remember, our God is a God who rules time and makes it serve His purposes, and He does this for our good. He can make the sun stop so that His people win a battle. He can make time move backward so that the shadow on a sundial reverses itself and keep the shoes of His people from wearing out, meaning He can stop the ravages of time. Our God rules time, and He does it on our behalf.

So what does that mean? It means our time is pregnant, that every hour we live is pregnant with meaning, purpose, and God's multiplication of time.

Purim is a feast that celebrates the victory described in the Book of Esther. You likely already know this story, but let's review it again together.

In the Persian Empire there was a king named Xerxes. He was the son of Darius the Great. His queen was Vashti, but she displeased him, and he took as his wife instead a beautiful Jewish maiden named Hadassah (Esther). The king loved his new queen very much, but he did not know that Esther was Jewish, since she kept this a secret from him.

Esther had a cousin named Mordecai, who was one of her advisors. Mordecai, a godly man, saw an evil man named Haman elevated to a high-ranking position by the king, but he would not bow to Haman. Haman was enraged by what he considered Mordecai's lack of respect for him, and he began plotting against all Jews. He convinced the king that the Jews were his enemies, and the king gave permission to Haman to do with the Jews as he pleased.

Mordecai learned of Haman's intentions and reported them to Esther. Mordecai also told her that God had put her in her position "for such a time as this" (Esther 4:14) so that she could deliver the Jews from the evil plots against them. It would mean, though, that Esther would have to tell the king she was Jewish. Doing that might cost her everything, even her life. She was a righteous woman, however, and concluded, "If I perish, I perish!" (Esther 4:16).

Esther arranged a banquet at which she intended to confront the evil Haman in front of the king. But before this banquet occurred, Haman became so enraged with Mordecai that he had a gallows built upon which he intended to hang Mordecai.

At her banquet Esther told the king of the vast conspiracy that would take even her life. When the king demanded to know who had set the conspiracy into motion, Esther declared, "The adversary and enemy is this wicked Haman!" (Esther 7:6).

Immediately the king ordered Haman executed on the very gallows he had built for Mordecai. Then the king gave Queen Esther the estates once owned by Haman. He appointed Mordecai to a high office in the empire, and Esther convinced her husband, the king, to spare the Jews and to issue an edict on their behalf.

Soon afterward the Jews arose against all their enemies. People of other nationalities helped them, and they triumphed completely. It was such a moment of victory that Mordecai instructed all the Jewish people to celebrate the Feast of Purim to honor God for the deliverance He wrought for His people. The date of this Purim would be the fourteenth of Adar—the pregnant month—and the people would observe it for all time.

This is the glorious story of the victory God brought about through a young Jewish woman named Esther. It is a thrilling story, and we ought to remember its lessons forever. Yet my purpose in recounting the story of Purim is to show you that the themes of this story and this feast are fulfilled for you in Jesus. Jesus is saying to you, even in Purim, "This Scripture is fulfilled in your hearing."

Let me tell you: for those who serve Jesus, there is going to be a hanging, because Jesus is your defender, because He loves you and watches over you, and because His glory is your rear guard. Jesus will destroy those who oppose you.

The very ones who conspire against you and build gallows to end your life will find that God is able to confuse their plans and destroy them with the very weapons they would have used on you. Oh, yes, there's going to be a hanging, and it will be a hanging of the ones who have intended to hang you!

And why? Because God is for you, because God intends good for you, because He has adopted you and made you His own. What He did for Esther, He will do for you. Yes, there is going to be a hanging! A hanging of every enemy arrayed against you.

In times pregnant with purpose, times of deadly threat, you—God's servant—are positioned to play a role. He will inspire you with an anointed voice to act courageously. He will come and save and deliver you at just the right moment.

I'm not talking about Esther. I'm talking about you. You are chosen. You are positioned. You are given anointed counsel, and you have the capacity for courageous action that delivers those of your generation. This is all true because of what Jesus has done in your life. Your time is pregnant. Your life is pregnant. And there is a power in you that enables you to do more than all you can ask or imagine.

The meaning of Purim grants us revelation that is fulfilled right now in Jesus Christ! It is the same with all the feasts of God. They are *mo'edim*—the sacred signs, revealed in sacred times with God, to fulfill His sacred purposes.

May the Lord God Almighty fulfill His every feast and sign in you!

Chapter 15

THE CULMINATION
OF ALL CREATION

*Look, I am coming soon! My reward is with Me to give to
each one according to his work. I am the Alpha and the
Omega, the Beginning and the End, the First and the Last.*

REVELATION 22:12–13

T HE STUDY OF GOD'S DIVINE ENCOUNTERS IS MORE THAN
just an historical review of what some consider to be arcane
and obsolete religious rituals. It offers all who care to give them
more than a casual glance a fascinating measure of insight into
the plans and purposes of God for each of us as we move into
a future filled with wonder and possibility. In addition to every
other benefit we receive by understanding the imagery and
symbolism of God's feasts (*mo'edim*), I firmly believe that God
Almighty is using them all to point us to an even greater conclusion. What lies ahead is an event in which all of us will play an
important part—and we are rushing toward it just as quickly as
the unlocked wheels of time can carry us.

Each of the pilgrimage feasts—Passover (Pesach), Pentecost
(Shavuot), and Tabernacles (Sukkot)—correspond to a major harvest season in Israel.

Passover in the spring was a celebration of the barley harvest. As we have seen, it was during the Passover season, specifically the Feast of Firstfruits, that a priest offered a sheaf of barley to the Lord in the temple, which represented the best of the harvest that was ready to be reaped. Acceptance of the sheaf represented acceptance of the entire harvest.

Passover, Firstfruits, and Unleavened Bread all found historical fulfillment in the crucifixion, death, burial, and resurrection of the Lord Jesus Christ, 1 Corinthians 15:20, "But now is Christ risen from the dead and become the first fruits of those who have fallen asleep." He was raised from the dead by the power of God as the firstfruits of an abundant harvest of souls that would appear before the heavenly throne. His acceptance there would mean the acceptance of all who would believe in Him as Savior and Lord.

I believe it is no coincidence that Jesus gathered twelve disciples (eleven, after the disobedience of Judas) together who were willing to follow Him and be prepared to continue His ministry after His resurrection and ascension back to heaven. This small group represented a sort of firstfruits—a small portion of the abundant harvest that was surely and shortly to come. They were all ordinary people just like you and me. They did not emerge from the ranks of the elite or the erudite. They were not well-known or recognized because of fame or wealth, but the living God used them in wondrous and supernatural ways. In the dark, ominous, prophetic days of Passover weekend prior to the Resurrection, there were only eleven of them, and they were devastated by the loss of their leader. They were plagued by serious doubts. Would they even be able to continue as a cohesive group as a result of the discouragement and depression they suffered?

Then came the news of the Resurrection and the greatest understatement of all Scripture is recorded. I know that the

Bible is true, for if there were any statement written there with the potential for exaggeration or overstatement, it is here. John 20:20 records it, "The disciples were then *glad* when they saw the Lord" (emphasis added). Jesus Himself appeared directly to them! He was alive, and suddenly anything was possible. Jesus stayed with them for forty additional days, continuing to instruct them regarding the principles of the kingdom of God and further preparing them for the work He intended for them accomplish.

The disciples were still uncertain concerning the nature of the kingdom of which Jesus spoke to them so often. They questioned the resurrected Christ on the day of His ascension if the kingdom was going to be restored at that time. Jesus assured them God alone knew that timetable and would not miss His appointment. "The Lord is not slack concerning his promise" (2 Peter 3:9, KJV).

Then the living Christ gave them what may have seemed like an unusual instruction. He specifically directed them to stay in Jerusalem until Pentecost, which by this time was little more than a week away. He informed them that He had something to give them on that specific day, and that they would be unprepared to fulfill His purpose for them without it.

Pentecost, as we have seen, was fifty days after Passover and was the second of the three feasts that required all Jewish men to present themselves before the Lord at the temple. By this time, the group of believers had grown, and one hundred twenty were present in a house in Jerusalem when the feast day came.

It was at Pentecost that the outpouring of the Holy Spirit prophesied by Joel occurred, and those present found themselves filled to overflowing with the same Holy Spirit that energized Jesus during His earthly ministry and in fact raised to life again the three-day-dead body of God's crucified Lamb! This was the promise the Lord Jesus had declared to them. That promise was gloriously and historically fulfilled as recorded in Acts 2:1–4.

Pentecost was the celebration of the wheat harvest in Israel. As I have mentioned, during this festival, two loaves of leavened bread were waved before the Lord, signifying that there would be a harvest that would go beyond the boundaries of the Hebrew nation to include the unleavened Gentile world as well. This was the purpose of the Pentecostal outpouring according to Acts 1:8: "But you shall receive power when the Holy Spirit comes upon you. And you shall be My witnesses in Jerusalem, and in all Judea and Samaria, and to the ends of the earth."

The plan and purpose of God included a logical progression from a small group of disciples at Passover to a much larger harvest of Jews and Gentiles at the Feast of Pentecost. The Book of Acts is a chronicle of how this magnificent gospel advanced far beyond the reaches and confines of the Jews in Jerusalem and Judea into the broader world, touching the Gentiles and transforming them by the power of Almighty God.

Pentecost has also had an historical fulfillment that we heard about in prophetic form in the Book of Joel and read about in real time in Acts 2. We are living in what Joel called a time of restoration, when God would pour out His Spirit on all flesh. It is a time of ingathering, a time of harvest. God has commissioned us to "go into all the world, and preach the gospel to every creature" (Mark 16:15). The Word of God is going out by every available means, and the reapers are engaged in harvest fields that a generation ago were unknown and unimaginable. Certainly there are significant challenges, but there have been obstacles to the proclamation of the gospel in every generation. Our responsibility and opportunity is to allow the divine "go" of Pentecostal wind to blow us next door and around the world, to allow the very breath of God to transport us across geographical, racial, gender, and religious barriers. We must allow that Holy Ghost hurricane to blow the props of self-dependence and religious ritual out from under our arms that we have used them as crutches for far too long! We must not allow anything static or stagnant to remain. We must stand, for sitting is a contented posture. Where we sit, we intend to stay. We must arise. We must go and tell everyone everywhere we find them the best news anyone could ever hear: "Jesus is coming soon. Get ready to meet Him through repentance and faith in His cross."

If that were the end of the story, it would be worthy of telling to every person in every generation. But as with everything related to God's kingdom, no matter how much you have seen or experienced, there is always more. And the more you see, the better it becomes. There is one more feast, the fall Feast of Tabernacles, that is awaiting its fulfillment, has not been historically manifested, and it involves the final harvest.

The fall season of Tabernacles (Sukkot) involves three feasts as well—Trumpets (Rosh Hashanah), the Day of Atonement (Yom Kippur), and the Feast of Tabernacles. It is also the time of ingathering of the fruits of the field in Israel, including figs, dates, olives, and most importantly grapes. As we have seen, this is the only feast season that has not had its historical fulfillment in the life and ministry of Jesus Christ. This prompting many to believe that when Jesus returns, it will be at this season of the year. Speculation has been heightened as I write this, since we are approaching the end of a Shemitah year and the beginning of a Jubilee year that corresponds with the fourth in a tetrad of Red Blood Moons, which will not occur again for approximately five hundred years.

Let me say with all sincerity and great certainty: I am not predicting that Jesus is coming back at a specific time. I am saying with confidence that I believe His appearing is imminent, and we need to make sure that as many people as possible are ready, because the final harvest is at hand.

Tabernacles was a time of tremendous celebration and great joy, as the people of God thanked Him for His abundant provision. They commemorated His presence by abiding in temporary tabernacles, reminiscent of the tents that Israel used during their track through the howling and harrowing wilderness from Egypt to the Promised Land. God was with them then, and He abides with us today. Tabernacles also marked the final harvest of the year—the culmination of all their labors and the certainty of sufficiency for the days ahead.

I want to reiterate this concept of harvests for a moment. Passover was the barley harvest, represented by a small group of disciples being made ready for their apostolic ministry. Pentecost was the wheat harvest, and that resulted in a larger group reaping in a larger field. But Tabernacles was the final harvest—the ultimate reaping—after which there was no more work to be accomplished in the fields. The Passover harvest has already been fulfilled. The Pentecost harvest—the reaping of the Gentile world—is underway. What could possibly be greater than that? What does God have in mind?

Jesus spoke, illuminating for us, this concept of an ultimate harvest in the parable of the wheat and the tares in Matthew 13. He talked of wheat and tares growing together until they are separated at harvest time. His disciples didn't quite understand it, so they asked Him to explain. Here is His response, from verses 37–43:

> He who sows the good seed is the Son of Man, the field is the world, and the good seed are the sons of the kingdom. But the weeds are the sons of the evil one. The enemy who sowed them is the devil, the harvest is the end of the world, and the reapers are the angels.
>
> Therefore as the weeds are gathered and burned in the fire, so shall it be in the end of this world. The Son of Man shall send out His angels, and they shall gather out of His

kingdom all things that offend, and those who do evil, and will throw them into a fiery furnace. There will be wailing and gnashing of teeth. Then the righteous will shine forth as the sun in the kingdom of their Father. Whoever has ears to hear, let him hear.

This reaping metaphor is found again, although with a different crop, in Revelation 14:14–16:

I looked. And there was a white cloud, and on the cloud sat One like a Son of Man, having on his head a golden crown, and in His hand a sharp sickle. Then another angel came out of the temple, crying with a loud voice to Him who sat on the cloud, "Thrust in Your sickle and reap. The time has come for You to reap, for the harvest of the earth is ripe." So He who sat on the cloud thrust His sickle on the earth, and the earth was harvested.

I believe that one of the reasons the Tabernacles harvest has been held back is that there is a great multitude of souls who need to be prepared for our Lord's return. This is our responsibility as believers, and we have a brief window of time to fulfill the commission we have received from our King. The last great Tabernacles harvest will be fulfilled, just as certainly as Passover and Pentecost were historically culminated—and I believe that the time is much nearer than we have believed.

All the feasts—all the signs in the heavens, all the celestial clues, and all the works and wonders of God—point to a great culmination that will be the final historic fulfillment of Tabernacles. Jesus will appear in the clouds, and gather His own to Himself, according to 1 Thessalonians 4:13–18 and 1 Corinthians 15:51–57. Seven years later He will return to this blue marble, people planet, accompanied by a multitude of saints who will return with Him to rule and reign. Then, according to Revelation 21:3: "And I heard a loud voice from heaven, saying, "Look! The tabernacle of God is with men, and He will dwell with them. They shall be His people, and God Himself will be with them and be their God."

When Jesus came into Jerusalem at the beginning of the final Passover He would celebrate on Earth, a great multitude accompanied Him in the way, praising God and hailing Him as their hero. That crowd was soon disillusioned and dispersed.

Jesus wept over the city and said these words in Matthew 23:37–39:

> O Jerusalem, Jerusalem, you who kill the prophets and stone those who are sent to you, how often I would have gathered your children together as a hen gathers her chicks under her wings, but you would not! Look, your house is left to you desolate. For I tell you, you shall not see Me again until you say, "Blessed is He who comes in the name of the Lord."

There will come a day when Jesus returns to Jerusalem not to the acclaim of fickle crowds of fair-weather followers but to those who are truly repentant and ready to receive Him. When He arrives, there will be another group who will accompany Him— the saints of all ages who are already in heaven will ride with Him, as prophesied in Revelation 19:11–16:

> I saw heaven opened. And there was a white horse. He who sat on it is called Faithful and True, and in righteousness He judges and wages war. His eyes are like a flame of fire, and on His head are many crowns. He has a name written, that no one knows but He Himself. He is clothed with a robe dipped in blood. His name is called The Word of God. The armies in heaven, clothed in fine linen, white and clean, followed Him on white horses. Out of His mouth proceeds a sharp sword, with which He may strike the nations. "He shall rule them with an iron scepter." He treads the winepress of the

fury and wrath of God the Almighty. On His robe and on His thigh He has a name written: KING OF KINGS AND LORD OF LORDS.

The ultimate Feast of Tabernacles and its historic fulfillment is rapidly approaching. The culmination of all creation is at hand. The trumpet blast of the last Jubilee is about to sound and echo around the globe. The final harvest is about to commence. Make all your preparations sure to receive your soon coming King.

This book is dedicated to my mother, Mrs. Ellen Parsley. Here is her favorite final days songs:

> The marketplace is empty
> No more traffic in the streets
> All the builders' tools are silent
> No more time to harvest wheat
> Busy housewives cease their labors
> In the courtroom no debate
> Work on earth has been suspended
> As the King comes through the gate.
>
> **CHORUS:**
> O the King is coming
> The King is coming
> I just heard the trumpet sounding
> And now His face I see
> O the King is coming
> The King is coming
> Praise God, He's coming for me.
>
> Happy faces line the hallways
> Those whose lives have been redeemed
> Broken homes that He has mended
> Those from prison He has freed

Little children and the aged
Hand in hand stand all aglow
Who were crippled, broken, ruined
Clad in garments white as snow.

I can hear the chariots rumble
I can see the marching throng
The flurry of God's trumpets
Spells the end of sin and wrong
Regal robes are now unfolding
Heaven's grandstand's all in place
Heaven's choir is now assembled
Start to sing "Amazing Grace."[1]

Understanding the *Feasts* of God

2 SEASONS, 3 DIVISIONS, 7 FEASTS

Spring
Former/Early Rain - *Historically Fulfilled Feasts*

Fall
Latter Rain - *Historically Unfulfilled Feasts*

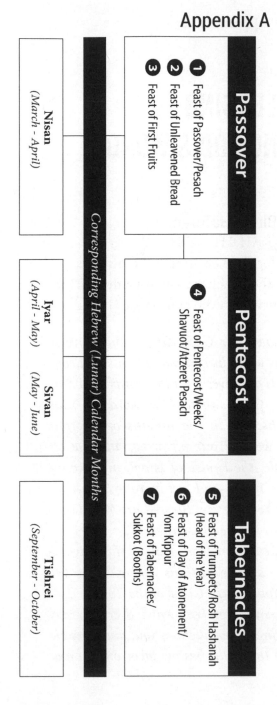

Passover
1. Feast of Passover/Pesach
2. Feast of Unleavened Bread
3. Feast of First Fruits

Pentecost
4. Feast of Pentecost/Weeks/ Shavuot/Atzeret Pesach

Tabernacles
5. Feast of Trumpets/Rosh Hashanah (Head of the Year)
6. Feast of Day of Atonement/ Yom Kippur
7. Feast of Tabernacles/ Sukkot (Booths)

Corresponding Hebrew (Lunar) Calendar Months

Nisan
(March - April)

Iyar
(April - May)

Sivan
(May - June)

Tishrei
(September - October)

Appendix B

A BLESSING FOR READING GOD'S WORD

Birkat HaTorah
(Beer-KAHT Ha-TOH-rah)
A Blessing for the Learning of Torah[1]
Recited as part of the Shacharit (shah-khah-REET),
which is the morning service in the synagogues of the world.[2]

Blessed art Thou, LORD our God, King of the universe, who has sanctified us with His commandments and commanded us to engross ourselves with the words of Torah.

Please LORD, our God, sweeten the words of Your Torah in our mouths and in the mouths of all Your people Israel. May we and our offspring, and the offspring of Your people, the House of Israel, may we all, together, know Your name and study Your Torah for the sake of fulfilling Your desire. Blessed are You, LORD, who teaches Torah to His people Israel.

Blessed are You, LORD our God, King of the universe, Who chose us from all the nations and gave us the Torah. Blessed are You, LORD, Giver of the Torah.

May the LORD bless you and keep watch over you; may the LORD make His presence enlighten you, and may He be kind to you; may the LORD bestow favor on you and grant you peace.

Appendix C

BLESSINGS, PRAYERS, AND SCRIPTURES FOR HEBREW CEREMONIES

THE PASSOVER SEDER

The Jewish observance of Passover (the Hebrew word is *Pesach*) centers on a Seder meal that includes readings from the Torah, object lessons, words from ancient rabbis, and even ritual questions asked by children. This ceremonial meal is defined in the Haggadah, "the telling," which is named in fulfillment of the charge in Exodus 13:8 that parents tell their children the story of God's preservation when death and the curse "passed over" the children of Israel in Egypt: "You shall declare to your son on that day, saying, 'This is done because of that which the LORD did for me when I came forth out of Egypt.'"

The blessings and prayers

The Passover Seder includes the following opening blessing:

> *Blessed are You, God, our God, King of the universe,*
> *who has chosen us from among all people, and raised*
> *us above all tongues, and made us holy through His*

commandments. And You, God, our God, have given us in love a holy convocation, commemorating the departure from Egypt. For You have chosen us and sanctified us from all the nations, and You have given us as a heritage Your holy Shabbat and Festivals in love and favor, in happiness and joy. Blessed are You, God, who sanctifies the Shabbat and Israel and the festive seasons.

During this Seder, four cups of wine are consumed, each commemorating one of four promises from Exodus 6:6–7:

Therefore say to the children of Israel: 'I am the LORD, and I will bring you out from under the burdens of the Egyptians, and I will rid you out of their bondage, and I will redeem you with a stretched-out arm and with great judgments. And I will take you to Me for a people, and I will be to you a God. And you shall know that I am the LORD your God, who brings you out from under the burdens of the Egyptians.

1. I will bring you out (the Cup of Consecration)

2. I will free you (the Cup of Deliverance).

3. I will redeem you (the Cup of Redemption).

4. I will take you as my own people (the Cup of Praise).

Remember that Jesus was performing this Seder meal with His disciples when He took the third cup of wine, the Cup of Redemption:

Then He took the cup, and after He gave thanks, He gave it to them, saying, "Drink of it, all of you. For this is My blood of the new covenant, which is shed for many for the remission of sins."

—MATTHEW 26:27–28

Among the many words from Scripture read during the Seder meal are these joyous words that recall the return of Israel from captivity in Babylon:

> When the LORD restored the captives of Zion, we were like those who dream. Then our mouth was filled with laughter, and our tongue with singing.
>
> Then they said among the nations, "The LORD has done great things for them."
>
> The LORD has done great things for us; we are glad. Restore our captives, O LORD, as the streams in the Negev. Those who sow in tears shall reap in joy. He who goes forth and weeps, bearing precious seed to sow, shall come home again with rejoicing, bringing his grain sheaves with him.

—PSALM 126

At the end of the Seder, this traditional prayer is spoken:

> *Blessed are You, Lord our God, King of the universe for the vine and the fruit of the vine, for the produce of the field, and for the precious, good and spacious land which You have favored to give as an heritage to our fathers, to eat of its fruit and be satiated by its goodness. Have mercy, Lord our God, on Israel Your people, on Jerusalem Your city, on Zion the abode of Your glory, on Your altar and on Your Temple. Rebuild Jerusalem, the holy city, speedily in our days, and bring us up into it, and make us rejoice in it, and we will bless You in holiness and purity and remember us for good on this day of the Festival of Matzo. For You, Lord, are good*

and do good to all, and we thank You for the land and for the fruit of the vine. Blessed are You, Lord, for the land and for the fruit of the vine.

Finally, there is the traditional chant, "Next year in Jerusalem!"

The texts

The texts read during Passover include the following:

- Exodus 12:1–4: The Passover Lamb

- Leviticus 23:5: The date for Passover

- Numbers 9:1–14; 28:16: Rules for the observance of Passover

- Deuteronomy 16:1–7: The description of unleavened bread

THE FEAST OF UNLEAVENED BREAD

The Feast of Unleavened Bread, or *Chag HaMatzot*, is part of Passover. Specifically the focus is on the eating of unleavened bread as a remembrance of the original Passover night.

The blessings and prayers

Because Passover and the Festival of Unleavened Bread are observed together as parts of a whole, the *Chag HaMatzot* blessings and prayers would be included in the Passover services above.

The texts

The texts read during Chag HaMatzot include the following:

- Exodus 12:21–51: The story of Passover

- Numbers 28:16–25: Rules for the observance of Passover

- Joshua 3:5–7, 5:2–6:1, 6:27: Passover in Canaan

THE FEAST OF FIRSTFRUITS

The Feast of Firstfruits, or *Reishit Katzir*, occurs the day after the Sabbath included in the Feast of Unleavened Bread.

The blessings and prayers

Reishit Katzir is part of Passover and is included in the Passover services described above. In addition, the priests bless the congregation with the priestly blessing during the Musaf prayer, which is the additional prayer service said during some holy days.

The texts

The texts read during the Feast of Firstfruits include the following:

- Exodus 33:12–34:26: Covenant promises to Israel

- Numbers 28:19–25: Rules for the seven days of Reishit Katzir

- 2 Samuel 22:1–51: David's song of deliverance

THE FEAST OF WEEKS

The Feast of Weeks, or *Shavuot*, occurs fifty days after Pesach and commemorates the giving of the Torah and the harvest of the firstfruits. The rabbis teach that the reason Shavuot is not on a particular date, but instead is marked by the counting from Passover, is to keep the remembrance of Passover always in the forefront.

Because the festival is a celebration of the giving of the Torah, it is traditional to stay up all night reading Scripture on the evening before the first day and then begin the first day of Shavuot with prayer. The holiday is marked by using decorations of greenery and eating dairy and sweets (milk and honey). Every evening includes a festive holiday meal.

The blessings and prayers

As the sun sets on the eve of Shavuot, candles are lit and this blessing is said:

> *Blessed are you, God, Our God, Sovereign of the Universe, who has made us holy with commandments and has commanded us to light the festival candles.*
>
> *And blessed you are, God, Our God, Sovereign of the Universe who has let us live and sustained us and has brought us to this time.*

A special holiday Kiddush (sanctification) is spoken before each meal:

> *Praised are You, Adonai our God, Ruler of the world, who creates the fruit of the vine.*

And then:

> *Praised are You, Adonai our God, Ruler of the world, who brings forth bread from the earth.*

The texts

The texts read during Shavuot include the following:

- Exodus 19–20: The giving of Torah to the Israelites
- Leviticus 23:15–21; Deuteronomy 16:9–12, 16–17: The specific rules for Shavuot

- The Book of Ruth: Included perhaps because it was during the spring harvest that Ruth was gleaning in the field of Boaz. Ruth became the grandmother of King David and therefore is an ancestor of Jesus.

THE FEAST OF TRUMPETS

Rosh Hashanah, which occurs in the fall on the first and second days of the Hebrew month of Tishrei, is one of the Jewish nation's holiest festivals and celebrates the creation of the world. Interestingly, the name "Rosh Hashanah" is not used in the Bible, but instead the holiday is called Yom Ha-Zikkaron (the Day of Remembrance) or Yom Teruah (the Day of the Sounding of the Shofar), and is instituted in Leviticus 23:24.

The holiday is filled with deep meaning and is the subject of thousands of pages of written text. Just a few aspects of the observance of Rosh Hashanah are acknowledging the sovereignty of God, spending time in contemplation and personal renewal, and offering prayers for the year to come. Jews around the world celebrate in many ways, including wearing new clothes, attending synagogue, and listening to the shofar (ram's horn) being blown.

Regular daily liturgy is expanded for Rosh Hashanah, and a special prayer book called the *machzor* is used for Rosh Hashanah and Yom Kippur because of the extensive liturgical changes required. A few of the special segments are below.

The blessings and prayers

> *We praise You, Eternal God, Sovereign of the Universe, who makes us holy with mitzvot and commands us to kindle the lights (of the Sabbath) and of the Day of Remembrance.*

Shehecheyanu: Who Has Kept Us Alive

> *Blessed are you, Lord, our God, sovereign of the universe*
> *Who has kept us alive, sustained us, and enabled us*
> *to reach this season.*

Special additional segments to the Rosh Hashanah service:

- Hamelech: Acknowledging God as sovereign

- Avinu Malkeinu: Acknowledging God as our Father and King

- Musaf for Rosh Hashanah: Prayer with three extra sections

- Malchuyot: Again focused on the sovereignty of God

- Zichronot: Remembrance, both God's remembrance of His covenants with His people, and the worshipper's remembrance of promises made

- Shofrot: The power of the shofar

The texts

The texts read during Rosh Hashanah include the following:

- Genesis 1: The creation of the world

- Genesis 21: The story of the miraculous birth of Isaac and God's promise to Sarah

- 1 Samuel: The answer to Hannah's prayer, the birth of a son, Samuel

- Genesis 22: Abraham's willingness to sacrifice his son Isaac

- Jeremiah 31: God's everlasting love for His people and the future ingathering of Israel's exiles

YOM KIPPUR

Yom Kippur, which occurs in the fall on the tenth day of the Hebrew month of Tishrei, is the most important holiday of the Jewish calendar. It commemorates the day when God forgave His people for creating and worshipping the golden calf. Yom Kippur, commanded in Leviticus 23:36, is the time set aside to atone for the sins of the past year. On Yom Kippur, the book that holds the record of those sins is sealed; therefore any chance to change that judgment by amending wrongs or repenting of sins ends at the close of the holiday.

Yom Kippur includes a complete fast of food and water, and for Orthodox Jews, even washing, using cosmetics and deodorants, and wearing leather clothing are prohibited. Traditionally, white clothing is worn, and the holiday is spent primarily in the synagogue for morning, afternoon, and evening services, which end with the sounding of the shofar.

The all-day services include far-reaching prayers of confession and supplication, including a prayer to annul unwise vows, confession of the sins of the community, and petitions for forgiveness, most of which involve repentance for the mistreatment of others.

The blessings and prayers

Kol Nidrei, more a proclamation than a prayer, this is spoken three times, from soft to loud:

All vows we are likely to make, all oaths and pledges we are likely to take between this Yom Kippur and the next Yom Kippur, we publicly renounce. Let them all be relinquished and abandoned, null and void, neither firm nor established. Let our vows, pledges and oaths be considered neither vows nor pledges nor oaths.

May all the people of Israel be forgiven, including all the strangers who live in their midst, for all the people are in fault.

O pardon the iniquities of this people, according to Thy abundant mercy, just as Thou forgave this people ever since they left Egypt.

The Lord said, "I pardon them according to your words."

Shehecheyanu Who Has Kept Us Alive

Blessed are You, Lord, our God, sovereign of the universe Who has kept us alive, sustained us, and enabled us to reach this season.

The texts

The texts read during Yom Kippur include the following:

- Leviticus 16:1–34: Description of the service performed by the high priest, the role of the scapegoat, and the atonement of sins for the Israelites

- Leviticus 18:1–30: Commandments against perverse sexual practices

- Isaiah 57:14–58:14: Assurance of God's forgiveness and comfort, and admonishment for a righteous fast and true observance of the Sabbath

- Book of Jonah: Jonah's rebellion, time spent in the belly of a whale, repentance, and mission

- Micah 7:18–20: God's delight in showing mercy

THE FEAST OF TABERNACLES

The Feast of Tabernacles, or *Sukkot*, is a weeklong fall celebration commemorating the Israelites' forty-year wandering in the wilderness. During this festival, Jews build and dwell in temporary shelters, imitating their ancestors' journey.

The blessings and prayers

Sukkot Kiddush

Kiddush is recited while holding a cup of wine or other liquid, no less than 3.3 ounces.

> *Blessed are You, Lord, our God, sovereign of the universe*
> *Who creates the fruit of the vine (Amen)*
> *Who made all things exist through His word (Amen)*
> *Blessed are You, Lord, our God, sovereign of the universe*
> *who has chosen us from among all people, and exalted us above every tongue and sanctified us with His commandments, and you gave us, Lord our God, with love appointed festivals for gladness, festivals and times for joy this day of the festival of Sukkot, the time of our gladness*
> *a holy convocation, a memorial of the exodus from Egypt*
> *because You have chosen us and made us holy from all peoples*
> *and Your holy festivals in gladness and in joy You have given us for an inheritance*
> *Blessed are You, Lord, who sanctifies Israel and the season.*

The blessing for dwelling in the Sukkah

This blessing should be recited at any time you are fulfilling the mitzvah of dwelling in the sukkah, for example, before you eat a meal in the sukkah.

> *Blessed are You, Lord, our God, sovereign of the universe*
>   *Who has sanctified us with His commandments and*
> *commanded us to dwell in the sukkah.*

Shehecheyanu Who Has Kept Us Alive

> *Blessed are You, Lord, our God, sovereign of the universe*
>   *Who has kept us alive, sustained us, and enabled us*
> *to reach this season.*

Drink the Kiddush wine after the Shehecheyanu blessing.

Farewell to the sukkah

This farewell blessing refers to the "hide of the Leviathan," because traditional Jewish teaching says that the giant sea creature will be slain when Messiah comes, and its hide used as a sukkah.

> *May it be Your will, Lord, our God and God of our*
> *ancestors that just as I have stood up and dwelled in*
> *this sukkah so may I merit next year to dwell in the*
> *sukkah of the hide of the Leviathan.*
>   *Next year in Jerusalem!*

The texts

The texts read during Sukkot include the following:

- Leviticus 22:26–23:44: The specific rules for Sukkot and other holidays

- Numbers 29:12–16: Other rules, and the description of the temple offerings for Sukkot

- Zachariah 14:1–21: A description of the end times

- Kings 8:2–21: The dedication of Solomon's temple

More information about all of the feasts and the liturgies of the feasts can be found at Chabad.org.

Appendix D

A GLOSSARY OF HEBREW TERMS

Counting of the Omer [OH-mer]: The counting of the days between Passover and Shavuot, announced daily during Passover along with a blessing; intended to remind Jews of the link between Passover, which commemorates the Exodus and Shavuot, which commemorates the giving of the Torah.

Days of Awe: The name for the ten days from Rosh Hashanah to Yom Kippur, a time for introspection and consideration of the sins of the previous year.

Feast of Firstfruits: This feast celebrates the first yield of the harvest in spring. It is comprised primarily of a wave offering of a sheaf of grain by a priest. There followed the sacrifice of a male lamb. This celebration reminded God's people of His provision for their every need.

Feast of Passover (or Pesach [PAY-sahk]): The first of three pilgrimage festivals with historical and agricultural significance. This feast commemorates the Jewish Exodus from Egypt in which God "passed over" the houses of the Jews that bore the blood of the sacrificial lamb on their doorposts.

Feast of Tabernacles (or Booths or Sukkot [soo-KOTE]): This is the third of three pilgrimage festivals with historical and agricultural significance. This feast commemorates the gathering of the harvest and God's provision for the people of Israel in their wilderness wanderings. Traditionally, Jews live in booths for one week to recall their deliverance from Egypt and subsequent wilderness journeys.

Feast of Weeks (or Pentecost or Shavuot [sha-voo-OHT]): This is the second of three pilgrimage festivals with historical and agricultural significance. This holiday commemorates the giving of the Torah at Mount Sinai and celebrates the spring harvest.

Hoshana Rabbah (hoe-SHAH-nah rah-BAH): Also known as the last of the Days of Judgment, which began on Rosh Hashanah, this is the seventh day of the Feast of Sukkot on which seven circuits are made around the synagogue reciting a prayer with the refrain, "Hoshana!" meaning, "Please save us!"

hyssop: The biblical use of this word refers to one of several herbs that have aromatic and cleansing properties, grow wild in Israel, and can easily be bunched together to be used for sprinkling in instances of religious purification. This hyssop was used to apply the blood of sacrificial animals.

Jubilee: Coming at the end of seven cycles of sabbatical years, the year of Jubilee—the fiftieth year—was one in which slaves were freed, debts were forgiven, and both land and people were granted rest.

kosher: Food that is permissible to eat under Jewish dietary laws. This term can also describe any other ritual object that is fit for use according to Jewish law.

lulav (LOO-lahv): A collection of palm, citron, myrtle, and willow branches used to fulfill the commandment to "rejoice before the Lord" during the Festival of Sukkot.

moed plural *mo'edim* (moh-EHD; moh-eh-DEEM): A Hebrew term that refers primarily to the five "festive seasons" of God. It means "festivals and set or appointed times" as well as to "signify" or "act as a sign."

Pesach Sheni (PAY-sahk SHAY-nee): A "Second Passover" for anyone who was unable to bring the offering on its appointed time. This occurs every year on 14 Iyar, exactly one month after 14 Nisan, which is the day before Passover.

Purim (poo-REEM): A Jewish holiday commemorating the deliverance of the Jewish people in the ancient Persian Empire. This deliverance is described in the Book of Esther.

rabbi: A religious teacher authorized to make decisions on issues of Jewish law. The term literally means "my master."

Rosh Hashanah (rahsh hah-SHAH-nah): Also called Feast of Trumpets. Literally the "head of the year," Rosh Hashanah marks the Jewish New Year. It is the first of the fall feasts that begin in the seventh month. It was marked by resting, blowing trumpets, having a holy convocation, and making offerings by fire to the Lord.

sage: A person of profound wisdom. Sages refers generally to the greatest Jewish minds of all times. Sometimes also referred to as Chazal, which is an acronym of the Hebrew phrase "Chachameinu Zichronam Liv'racha," meaning "our sages of blessed memory." In its strictest sense, Chazal refers to the final opinions expressed in the Talmud but is sometimes used more loosely to refer to the generally accepted opinion of any of the wise people who have contributed to Jewish law.

Seder (SAY-duhr): A ritual performed by a community or by multiple generations of a family, involving a retelling of the story of the liberation of the Israelites from slavery in ancient Egypt found in the Book of Exodus.

Shemini Atzeret (SHMEE-nee aht-ZEH-reht): Meaning "Eighth Day of Assembly," this holiday is distinct from, yet connected to, the Festival of Sukkot and serves as an opportunity for the Jewish people to spend extra time with God after Sukkot.

Shemitah (SHMIH-tah): The seventh year of the seven-year agricultural cycle mandated by the Torah and still observed in contemporary Judaism. During Shemitah, the land is left to lie fallow, and all agricultural activity, including plowing, planting, pruning and harvesting, is forbidden.

shofar (show-FAHR): A ram's horn, blown like a trumpet usually as a summons to the people. Shofars are used in Scripture to summon God's people to repentance, war, worship, and rest.

siddur (see-DOOR): A Jewish prayer book, containing a set order of daily prayers.

Simchat Torah (SEEM-kaht TOH-rah): Concurrent with Shemini Atzeret and meaning "Rejoicing in the Torah," this holiday marks the completion of the annual cycle of weekly Torah readings.

Talmud (TAL-mood): The collection of Jewish law and tradition consisting of the Mishnah and the Gemara and being either the edition produced in Palestine AD c400 or the larger, more important one produced in Babylonia AD c500.

tetrad: A series of four consecutive total lunar eclipses occurring at approximately six-month intervals.

Torah (TOH-rah): Meaning "instruction" or "teaching." In its narrowest sense, the Torah is the first five books of the Bible: Genesis, Exodus, Leviticus, Numbers, and Deuteronomy, sometimes called the Pentateuch or the Five Books of Moses. In its broadest sense, the Torah is the entirety of Jewish teachings, written and oral.

trumpets: Often *shofars* (ram horns), trumpets are used for summoning the congregation, sounding an alarm, going to war, and in worshipping God. See also: *Rosh Hashanah*.

unleavened bread: Also known as *matzo*, this bread without yeast is served during Passover, the festival celebrating the Exodus from Egypt. The Israelites left Egypt in such haste they could not wait for their bread dough to rise. The bread, when baked, was *matzo*. *Matzo* also symbolizes redemption and freedom, while serving as a reminder to be humble and not forget what life was like in servitude.

Yom Kippur (yohm kee-POOR): Also called Day of Atonement. A day set aside for fasting, depriving oneself of pleasures, and repenting from the sins between men and God during the previous year. Yom Kippur occurs on the tenth day of Tishrei and completes the annual period known as the *Yamim Nora'im* (Days of Awe) that commences with Rosh Hashanah.

THE JEHOVAH
NAMES OF GOD

T HE BIBLE TELLS US IN NO UNCERTAIN TERMS THAT THE name of God carries earth-shattering power. His name conveys His glory. His name conveys His character. His name conveys His irresistible strength. To draw close to God and to know Him intimately, it is important to learn His names. Our English words for God do not carry the detail and nuance that the Hebrew names for God do. We should learn these Hebrew names and use them as we pray, worship, and declare His will on Earth as it is being done in heaven.

Make it your goal to memorize as many of these names as you can. Meditate on them. Use them often. Most of all, allow them to paint a more accurate and transforming picture of who God is on your heart. Doing this will set you on the course of a deeply God-centered life, and it will help you view God through a more biblically Hebraic lens.

- Jehovah—the Lord (Exodus 6:2–3)

- Adonai Jehovah—the Lord God (Genesis 15:2)

- Jehovah Adon Kal Ha'arets—Lord of All the Earth (Joshua 3:11)

- Jehovah Bara—the Lord Creator (Isaiah 40:28)

- Jehovah Chassidi—the God of Mercy (Psalm 59:1)

- Jehovah Chayil—the God of Pentecost and Strength (Habakkuk 3:19)

- Jehovah Chezeq—the Lord My Strength (Psalm 18:1)

- Jehovah Chereb—the Lord the Sword (Deuteronomy 33:29)

- Jehovah El Gemuwal—the God of Recompense (Psalm 59:10)

- Jehovah Eli—the Lord My God (Psalm 18:2)

- Jehovah Elyon—the Lord Most High (Genesis 14:18)

- Jehovah 'EzoLami—the Lord My Strength (Psalm 28:7)

- Jehovah Gador Milchamah—the Lord Mighty in Battle (Psalm 24:8)

- Jehovah Ganan—the Lord Our Defense (Psalm 89:18)

- Jehovah Go'el—the Lord Thy Redeemer (Isaiah 49:26; 60:16)

- Jehovah Hamelech—the Lord the King (Psalm 98:6)

- Jehovah Hashopet—the Lord the Judge (Judges 11:27)

- Jehovah Hoshe'ah—the Lord Saves (Psalm 20:9)

- Jehovah 'Immeku—the Lord Is With You (Judges 6:12)

- Jehovah 'Izoz Hakaboth—the Lord Strong and Mighty (Psalm 24:8)

- Jehovah Jireh—the Lord Will Provide (Genesis 22:14)

- Jehovah Kabodhi—the Lord My Glory (Psalm 3:3)

- Jehovah Kanna—the Lord Whose Name Is Jealous (Exodus 34:14)

- Jehovah Kereno Yish'l—the Lord the Horn of My Salvation (Psalm 18:2)

- Jehovah Machsi—the Lord My Refuge (Psalm 91:9)

- Jehovah Magen—the Lord the Shield (Deuteronomy 33:29)

- Jehovah Ma'oz—the Lord My Fortress (Jeremiah 16:19)

- Jehovah Melech 'Olam—the Lord King Forever (Psalm 10:16)

- Jehovah Mephalti—the Lord My Deliverer (Psalm 18:2)

- Jehovah M'gaddishcem—the Lord Our Sanctifier (Exodus 31:13)

- Jehovah Misqabbi—the Lord My High Tower (Psalm 18:2)

- Jehovah Naheh—the Lord that Smiteth (Ezekiel 7:9)

- Jehovah Nissi—the Lord Our Banner (Exodus 17:15)

- Jehovah Nose—the God that Forgives (Psalm 99:8)

- Jehovah 'Ori—the Lord My Light (Psalm 27:1)

- Jehovah Perazin—the Lord Is Thy Breakthrough (2 Samuel 5:20)

- Jehovah Rapha—the Lord that Healeth (Exodus 15:26)

- Jehovah Rohi—the Lord My Shepherd (Psalm 23:1)

- Jehovah Saboath—the Lord of Hosts (1 Samuel 1:3)

- Jehovah Sel'l—the Lord My Rock (Psalm 18:2)

- Jehovah Shalom—the Lord Our Peace (Judges 6:24)

- Jehovah Shammah—the Lord Is There (Ezekiel 48:35)

- Jehovah Tsidkenu—the Lord Our Righteousness (Jeremiah 23:6)

- Jehovah Tsori—the Lord My Strength (Psalm 19:14)

- Jehovah 'Uzam—the Lord Their Strength (Psalm 37:39)

- Jehovah Yasha—the Lord Thy Savior (Isaiah 49:26; 60:16)

NOTES

CHAPTER 1:
UNDERSTANDING GOD'S TIMING

1. Abraham Joshua Heschel, "Shabbat as a Sanctuary in Time," MyJewishLearning.com, http://www.myjewishlearning.com/article /shabbat-as-a-sanctuary-in-time/ (accessed June 30, 2015).

2. Biblehub.com, s.v. *"moed,"* http://biblehub.com/hebrew/4150 .htm (accessed June 30, 2015).

3. James M. Johnston, "Catechism of the Jew Is His Calendar," *Milwaukee Sentinel*, September 23, 1967, http://tinyurl.com /pnrdv25 (accessed June 30, 2015).

4. M. H. Abrams and Geoffrey Galt Harpham, *A Glossary of Literary Terms* (Stamford, CT: Cengage Learning, 2015), 182.

CHAPTER 2:
THE PATTERN OF GOD'S CALENDAR

1. *Judaism* ed. Arthur Hertzberg (New York: The Free Press, 1991), 183.

2. Matthew 26:2; Mark 14:1, Luke 22:15; John 11:55; 1 Corinthians 5:7–8, to name a few.

3. Reuven Hammer, *Entering the High Holy Days: A Complete Guide to the History, Prayers, and Themes* (Philadelphia, PA: The Jewish Publication Society, 1998), 17.

4. "Quotes on the Meaning of Yom Kippur," *Algemeiner*, http:// www.algemeiner.com/2014/10/03/quotes-on-the-meaning-of-yom -kippur/ (accessed June 30, 2015).

5. Ibid.

CHAPTER 3:
RED BLOOD MOONS—BLIGHT OR BLESSING?

1. Jonathan Bernis, *A Rabbi Looks at Jesus of Nazareth* (Bloomington, MN: Chosen Books, 2011), 66.

2. Gopi Chandra Kharel, "Yom Kippur 2014: 15 Quotes, Wishes and Prayers to Celebrate the Jewish Festival, 'Day of Atonement,'"

International Business Times, October 3, 2014, http://www.ibtimes
.co.in/yom-kippur-2014-15-quotes-wishes-prayers-celebrate-jewish
-festival-day-atonement-610485 (accessed June 30, 2015).

3. Tony Phillips, "Total Lunar Eclipse," NASA.gov, http://www
.nasa.gov/vision/universe/watchtheskies/13oct_lunareclipse.html
(accessed June 23, 2015).

4. There is voluminous information regarding lunar eclipses at
NASA.gov and specific data about their occurrence in history can
be found at http://eclipse.gsfc.nasa.gov/LEcat5/appearance.html.

5. Ibid.

6. Ibid.

7. Ibid.

8. Ibid.

9. Ibid.

10. Ibid.

11. "What happened on the Ninth of Av?" Chabad.org, http://
www.chabad.org/library/article_cdo/aid/946703/jewish/What
-happened-on-the-Ninth-of-Av.htm (accessed June 23, 2015).

12. Michael Casey, "Jupiter, Venus to Converge in Star of Bethlehem Moment," CBS News, June 29, 2015, http://www.cbsnews
.com/news/jupiter-venus-to-converge-in-star-of-bethlehem
-moment/ (accessed June 30, 2015).

13. "Lunar Eclipses of 2015," NASA, http://eclipse.gsfc.nasa.gov
/lunar.html (accessed June 23, 2015).

CHAPTER 4:
FREEDOM IS YOURS

1. John J. Parsons, "Worthy Is the Lamb," Hebrew for Christians,
2012, http://www.lojsociety.org/H4C_Passover_Seder.pdf (accessed
June 30, 2015).

2. John J. Parsons, "Introduction to the Jewish Calendar," http://
www.hebrew4christians.com/Holidays/Calendar/calendar.html
(accessed June 23, 2015).

3. Rod Parsley, *The Cross* (Lake Mary, FL: Charisma House,
2013), 58.

4. Ibid., 59.

5. Ibid, 70.
6. Pesahim 7:13.
7. Parsley, *The Cross*, 90.

CHAPTER 5:
SECOND CHANCES ARE GOD'S SPECIALTY

1. David A. Teutsch, "Leaving Egypt," April 9, 2014, http://www
.huffingtonpost.com/rabbi-david-a-teutsch/leaving-egypt_b_5118319
.html? (accessed June 30, 2015).

CHAPTER 7:
DEAD THINGS CAN LIVE AGAIN

1. *Book of Common Prayer 1979 Edition* (New York: Oxford University Press, 1979), 364.

CHAPTER 8:
HOLY SPIRIT, COME!

1. Charles Haddon Spurgeon, "Life More Abundant," Spurgeon's Sermons, vol. 20: 1874, No. 1150.
2. A. W. Tozer, *Born After Midnight* (Camp Hill, PA: Christian Publications, 1992), 7.

CHAPTER 9:
STARTING OVER

1. "Great Quotes on the Meaning of Rosh Hashanah," *Algemeiner*, http://www.algemeiner.com/2014/09/19/great-quotes-on
-the-meaning-of-rosh-hashanah/ (accessed June 30, 2015).
2. Dovid Rosenfeld, "The Forgotten Supper," Aish.com, http://
www.aish.com/h/hh/yom-kippur/theme/the-forgotten-supper.html
(accessed June 30, 2015).
3. RabbiDebra.com, "Quotations & Commentary on Repentance and Forgiveness," http://www.rabbidebra.com/HHquotes
-commentaries.html (accessed June 30, 2015).
4. Irving Greenberg, *The Jewish Way: Living the Holidays* (New York: Touchstone, 1988), 99.

CHAPTER 12:
DWELLING WITH GOD

1. Hope of Israel Ministries, "A New Understanding of Shemini Atzeret—the 'Eighth Day,'" Hope-of-Israel.org, http://www.hope-of-israel.org/atzeret.html (accessed June 23, 2015).

CHAPTER 13:
THE EMBRACE OF GOD

1. Parsley, *The Cross*, 29–30; YouTube.com, "Brennan Manning on God's Love," uploaded by camister69, October 14, 2011, http://www.youtube.com/watch?v=0dMwu1rhTCQ (accessed July 7, 2015).

CHAPTER 15
THE CULMINATION OF ALL CREATION

1. "The King Is Coming" by Charles Millhuff, William Gaither, and Gloria Gaither. Copyright © 1970 Hanna Street Music (BMI) (adm. at CapitolCMGPublishing.com) All rights reserved. Permission requested.

APPENDIX B:
A BLESSING FOR READING GOD'S WORD

1. The word *torah* (TOH-rah) literally means "teaching" or "instruction." Though the word is commonly used to describe the first five books of the Old Testament, it can also mean the whole of God's revelation to His people and thus can be used by both Christians and Jews as a term for God's word or truth.

2. "Birkat HaTorah—Blessing for the Learning of Torah," Hebrew for Christians, http://www.hebrew4christians.com/Prayers/Daily_Prayers/Birkat_HaTorah/birkat_hatorah.html (accessed July, 2015).